Majors Exploration

A Search and Find Guide
for College and Career Direction

Diane Lindsey Reeves

Mary Jane Bradbury

Prentice Hall
Upper Saddle River, New Jersey 07458

Library of Congress Cataloging-in-Publication Data

Reeves, Diane Lindsey, 1959–
        Majors exploration : a search and find guide for college and
    career direction / Diane Lindsey Reeves, Mary Jane Bradbury.
            p.   cm.
        Includes index.
        ISBN 0-13-011379-4
            1. College majors—United States—Handbooks, manuals, etc.
    2. Vocational guidance—United States—Handbooks, manuals, etc.
    3. Field work (Educational method)—Handbooks, manuals, etc.
        I. Bradbury, Mary Jane.   II. Title.
        LB2361.5.R426   1999
        378.1'9425—dc21   98–47211
                                                                                    CIP

Publisher: *Carol Carter*
Acquisitions Editor: *Sue Bierman*
Managing Editor: *Mary Carnis*
Production: *Holcomb Hathaway, Inc.*
Production Liaison: *Glenn Johnston*
Director of Manufacturing and Production: *Bruce Johnson*
Manufacturing Buyer: *Marc Bove*
Cover Design: *Wanda España*
Editorial Assistant: *Michelle M. Williams*
Marketing Manager: *Jeff McIlroy*
Marketing Assistant: *Barbara Rosenberg*

© 1999 by Prentice-Hall, Inc.
Simon & Schuster / A Viacom Company
Upper Saddle River, New Jersey 07458

Printed in the United States of America

10 9 8 7 6 5 4 3 2 1

I S B N   0 - 1 3 - 0 1 1 3 7 9 - 4

Prentice-Hall International (UK) Limited, *London*
Prentice-Hall of Australia Pty. Limited, *Sydney*
Prentice-Hall Canada Inc., *Toronto*
Prentice-Hall Hispanoamericana, S.A., *Mexico*
Prentice-Hall of India Private Limited, *New Delhi*
Prentice-Hall of Japan, Inc., *Tokyo*
Simon & Schuster Asia Pte. Ltd., *Singapore*
Editora Prentice-Hall do Brasil, Ltda., *Rio de Janeiro*

CONTENTS

Introduction: The Adventure Begins! v

INTRODUCTION

The Adventure Begins!

At its best, a college education should provide the foundation for a lifetime of success and satisfaction in a vocation that makes the most of your interests, abilities, and values. It can be an adventure that stimulates your mind, broadens your horizons, and prepares you to fulfill lifelong ambitions. That's why choosing a college major is not a matter to be taken lightly. Frankly speaking, there is too much at stake to choose a major via the ever popular "eenie, meanie, miney, mo" method.

That's the method that a lot of students use to get their parents off their back or to have something to say when someone asks them what their major is. They simply pick the first thing that pops into their head or choose the most popular option and head toward graduation. The problem with this method, besides the countless hours and tons of money that you'll waste, is that you won't be any more equipped to take on your future when you graduate than you are right now. So, why bother?

Perhaps a better route would be to carefully examine your options and make a decision based on your own (and nobody else's!) interests, abilities, ambitions, and values. That way you'll be ready to pursue your dreams and make the most of the opportunities that come your way. Instead of floundering around, you'll have purpose and direction for your future and each class you take will provide a meaningful link for getting you where you want to go. What a concept!

The purpose of this guide is to provide the tools that you need to answer the question "Which major should I choose?" Use it to work through this all-important decision and to make the most of your college education.

Here's how it works. To get started, take a look at the table of contents. You'll notice that the college majors are grouped according to three broad disciplines: sciences, humanities and social sciences, and business. If you already have an inkling of which of these areas you like best, go directly to that section. If not, start at the beginning and start working your way through the options. In each chapter, you'll find in-depth information about that major, including:

- A description of the major
- Interesting history and background information
- A list of typical course requirements
- Ideas about how the degree relates to the workplace
- Advice from experts in the field

Along with this information, you'll also find several tools to help you apply the information to your individual circumstances. First, you'll find a series of questions that together pose the question *"Is This Major for You?"* Answer them as a means to gauge your interest in a particular field. If you answer *no* more than you answer *yes,* move on to another chapter that seems like a better fit.

Toward the end of each chapter, you'll find a section called *Before You Decide*. This section provides ideas and resources for completing four activities. Together, these four activities comprise a Field Research project that you'll be asked to complete. The activities are:

- Talk About It
- Read About It
- Experience It
- Explore the Options

Finally, each chapter concludes with a *Field Research Worksheet*. Once you come across a major that sounds promising, use this worksheet to plan a thorough investigation. To complete the worksheet you'll need to:

- Identify three people to interview.
- Find some books or Internet resources to read for more career-specific information.
- Schedule a tour or job-shadowing experience at a place that utilizes the skills and knowledge that this major provides.
- Look into specific career options related to the major.

Once you've narrowed down your interests and made a plan, move on to Part 5 of the book, where you'll find worksheets and other resources for each of the Field Research projects. Complete each activity to the best of your ability. Armed with all the facts, you can better decide if a particular major is right for you.

Mind you, this might not be the easiest task you've undertaken, but it's sure to be one that's worthwhile. Just remember to keep your options open, enjoy the process, and let the adventure begin!

1 Sciences

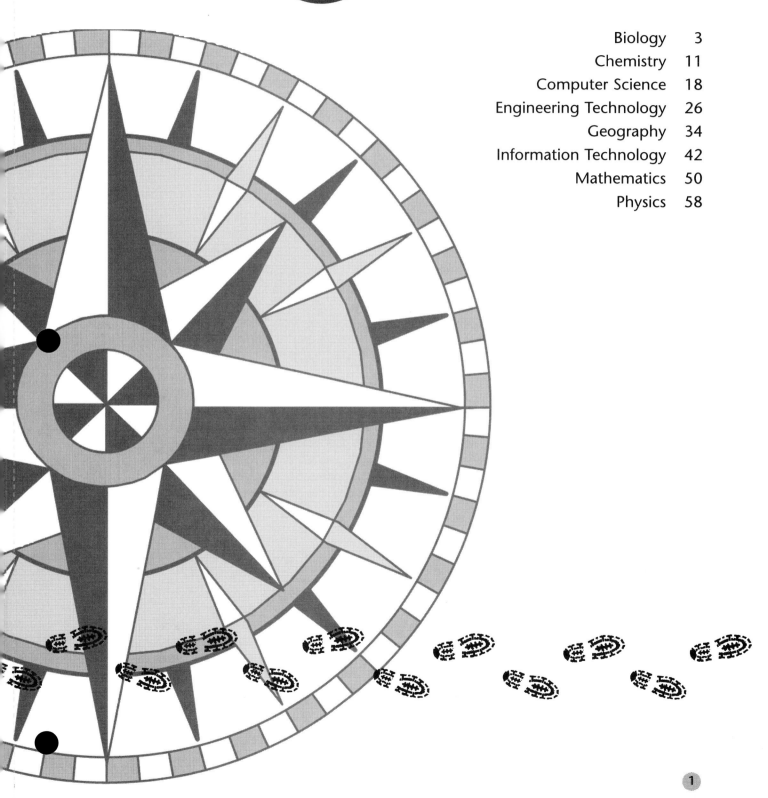

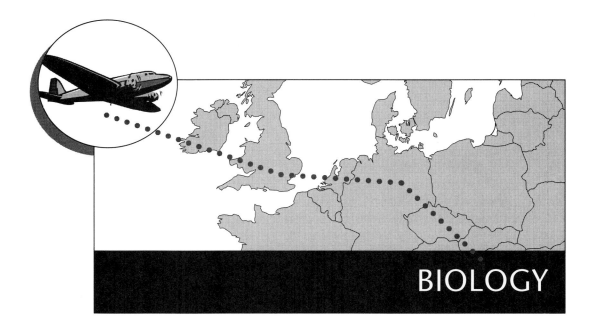

BIOLOGY

Is This Major for You?

- Are you interested in learning more about humans, plants, and animals?
- Would you enjoy working in a lab as most biologists do or would you prefer working closer to nature in an outdoor setting?
- Does specialization in an area such as botany, marine biology, or zoology appeal to you?
- Do you have a fascination with uncovering the secrets of life?
- Would you find the process of assembling the pieces of "nature's puzzle" something that could hold your interest for long periods of time?
- Are you good at thinking your way through various situations and problems?
- Is using scientific knowledge to find solutions for health concerns and other quality-of-life issues of importance to you?

If you answered yes to several of these questions, keep reading and find out if a major in biology is a good choice for you.

INTRODUCTION

Have you ever walked in the park? All around you are amazing signs of life—birds and squirrels that scurry along branches; trees, bushes, and grass that cover the ground; insects that hum in the background. These are the obvious ones. There is also an entire community of microscopic organisms that thrives unseen in the soil, organisms that have remained nearly unchanged for billions of years. How did this astonishing variety of living things evolve on Earth? In what ways do they interact with each other? What processes must occur for them to survive

Dr. Gerald Audesirk, Biology Professor at the University of Colorado, contributed to this article.

in their environments and reproduce? What processes do you, as a living creature, need in order to survive? The answers to these captivating questions are explored in the fascinating field of biology.

WHAT IS BIOLOGY?

Biology is the study of living things, from the most obvious—animals and plants—to the hidden—a virus that can reproduce itself inside a body, but has no living properties when isolated outside the host. Biology is probably the most diverse of all the sciences. While some biologists are creating new forms of life by manipulating genetic material, others are probing the workings of the brain, tracing the complex interactions within the ecosystems, or seeking new forms of life from the tropical rain forest to the ocean floor.

HISTORY AND BACKGROUND

The word *biology* comes from the Greek *bio* (life or living) and *logos* (the study of). Early Greek philosophers gathered many facts about plants and animals; one, Anaximander, went so far as to hypothesize that human beings evolved from fish! During the late Renaissance, interest in biology grew with many new discoveries: Belgian physician Vesalius (1514–1564) studied the human body and became the father of anatomy; Dutch scientist Antonie van Leeuwenhoek (1632–1723) used an early microscope and discovered bacteria; English scientist Robert Hooke (1635–1703) first described cells.

Throughout the 1800s discoveries and theories abounded, each further defining the many areas of biology that exist today. Gregor Mendel (1822–1884) discovered the principles of heredity. Louis Pasteur (1822–1895) proved that bacteria spread disease. In 1859, Charles Darwin revolutionized field biology with his theories about evolution. Evolution is the most important concept in biology. It is the theory that modern organisms descended, with modification, from preexisting life forms. Evolution occurs as a consequence of (1) *genetic variation* among members of a population, caused by mutation; (2) *inheritance* of those variations by offspring; and (3) *natural selection* of the variations that best adapt the organism to its environment. The result of evolution is a tremendous variety of species that have complex interrelationships with one another and with their nonliving surroundings.

BIOLOGY TODAY

Biology today is an incredibly diverse field, with individuals working on everything from the molecules of genetics to the interaction among populations of organisms. Traditionally the two major areas of biology are botany—the study of plants, and zoology—the study of animals. Many biological sciences, however, include both, and are interrelated in some way. The following are main areas in the field of biology.

ANATOMY. Study of the structure of plants and animals

BIOCHEMISTRY. Study of the chemistry of plants and animals, including microbiology, bacteriology, histology (tissues), cytology (cells), and enzymology

BIOLOGICAL PSYCHOLOGY. Application of biology to psychology, including genetics, human engineering, cybernetics (relationships between living things and mechanical devices), and organic evolution

BIOPHYSICS. Application of biology to physics, including cryobiology (living things in extremely cold surroundings)

ECOLOGY. Study of relationships of plants and animals to each other and to their environment, including biosociology and biogeography

EVOLUTIONARY BIOLOGY. Study of processes by which evolution generates life and the diversity of living things

EVOLUTIONARY PSYCHOLOGY. Study of how the behaviors of people affect the processes of life

GENETICS. Study of genes and how they affect structure and behavior of organisms

IMMUNOLOGY. Study of the defenses of the body against disease

MICROBIOLOGY. Study of microbes (e.g., bacteria and viruses) and how they live

PHYSIOLOGY. Study of normal functions of living things, including pharmacology, endocrinology, and embryology

TAXONOMY. Classification and naming of living things

WHAT COURSES DO YOU NEED TO TAKE?

Courses generally required for basic biology include:

Anatomy and Physiology	General Chemistry
Cell Biology	Genetics
Ecology	Organic Chemistry
General Biology	Physics

Recommended courses include statistics, biochemistry, and computer competency.

WHAT CAN YOU DO WITH A DEGREE IN BIOLOGY?

Most individuals use an undergraduate degree in biology for a background to further their education for health careers in medicine, physical therapy, dentistry, and optometry, to name a few. A bachelor's degree in biology with a teaching certification qualifies you to teach at the middle school and high school levels. Many undergraduates are employed as lab technicians for hospitals, medical schools, and pharmaceutical companies. At the local, state, and federal levels, governments hire biology majors for positions with the forest service, fish and wildlife divisions, and the Bureau of Land Management. In addition, private industries employ biology majors to monitor environmental concerns, such as factory locations and waste dumping.

WHAT DO EXPERTS SAY ABOUT BIOLOGY?

What can a person expect during the course of study? Students can expect a very challenging curriculum including chemistry and physics. The number of people who work for labs far exceeds the number walking in the woods discovering new insects. A strong chemistry background is necessary to meet the diverse demands of the discipline today.

What are the characteristics of a successful student? A successful student will be strong in the sciences and be able to combine memorization of names and facts with critical thinking. He won't be able to do much with the facts if he can't think about their role in the processes.

What do you see for the future of the discipline? The future of the discipline is wide open and there is much to do. Many areas are growing quite rapidly. For example, they will soon complete the entire DNA sequence of human genome—but that's just the beginning. This piece of information is like knowing the alphabet; we then go on and learn every word in the dictionary! Once we have the sequences in hand, how do we apply them to the human processes? Another area is the environment. How should we best design parks and refuges to preserve the diversity of the species? Lewis Thomas, physician and natural philosopher, describes our situation this way: "The only solid piece of scientific truth about which I feel totally confident is that we are profoundly ignorant about nature. Indeed, I regard this as the major discovery of the past hundred years of biology . . . but we are making a beginning."

What makes this field exciting to you, personally, and why do you love what you do? I am passionate about this field because it is exciting to see students opening their minds and working through complicated questions. Each year I teach, a student thinks of something that I've never thought of before. In research, there is an incredible thrill that accompanies discovery—to find something that no one knew before. Because biology deals with living organisms, it is all the more exciting.

BEFORE YOU DECIDE . . .

Before you invest the next four years pursuing this field of study, invest a few hours in a thorough investigation of what a degree in biology can do for you. Use the following suggestions and the worksheet at the end of this chapter to make a plan for conducting some field research. Once your plan is complete and approved by your instructor, proceed to Part 5, Field Research, where you'll find further instructions for making the most of these activities.

TALK ABOUT IT

Conduct interviews with the following three people (using the information included in the Field Research section in Part 5 to guide your discussions):

- A senior completing a degree in biology
- A biology professor at your school
- A professional working in a biology-related career

READ ABOUT IT

Following is a book listing that provides an overview of possible career options for someone with a degree in biology.

- Brown, Sheldon. *Opportunities in Biotechnology Careers.* Lincolnwood, IL: VGM Career Horizons, 1994.
- Czerneda, Julie. *Great Careers for People Interested in Living Things.* Detroit: Gale Research Inc., 1993.
- Easton, Thomas. *Careers in Science.* Indianapolis, IN: JIST, 1990.
- Goldberg, Jan. *Real People Working in Science.* Lincolnwood, IL: VGM Career Horizons, 1998.
- Janovy, John. *On Becoming a Biologist.* New York: Harper and Row, 1985.
- *Job Choices in Science and Engineering.* Bethlehem, PA: National Association of Colleges and Employers, 1998.
- Miller, Louise. *Careers for Nature Lovers and Other Outdoor Types.* Lincolnwood, IL: VGM Career Horizons, 1992.
- Morgan, Bradley J. and Joseph M. Palmisano, eds. *Physical Sciences Career Directory.* Detroit: Visible Ink Press, 1994.
- Vleck, Ronald B. *Life Sciences Jobs Handbook.* Gaithersburg, MD: Prospect Press, 1982.
- Winter, Charles. *Opportunities in Biological Sciences.* Lincolnwood, IL: VGM Career Horizons, 1990.

EXPERIENCE IT

Seek out an opportunity to see what a degree in biology can do for you in the workplace. Arrange a tour, a job-shadowing experience, or even a full-fledged internship at a place such as

- A pharmaceutical laboratory
- A hospital biotechnology laboratory
- A government research facility
- An agricultural research facility or cooperative extension office
- A food processing facility
- A veterinary clinic
- The newborn nursery at a zoo

Once you have scheduled a first appointment, use the information included in the Field Research section to make the most of this experience.

EXPLORE THE OPTIONS

Using the materials included in the Field Research section, conduct a thorough investigation of at least two career options for college graduates with a biology degree. You'll need a good selection of career books and resources and access to the Internet to complete this task.

Here are some ways to put a degree in biology to work. Use this list for ideas, but feel free to focus your exploration on another idea that interests you.

- Biochemist
- Biologist
- Botanist
- College Professor
- Ecologist
- Food Scientist
- Geneticist
- Health Care Consultant
- Horticulturist
- Immunologist
- Journalist

- Lab Technician
- Life Scientist
- Medical Technologist
- Microbiologist
- Pharmaceutical Salesperson
- Pharmacist
- Physician
- Physiologist
- Research Scientist
- Veterinarian
- Zoologist

REFERENCE

Audesirk, Gerald. *Biology: Life on Earth.* Upper Saddle River, NJ: Prentice Hall, 1996.

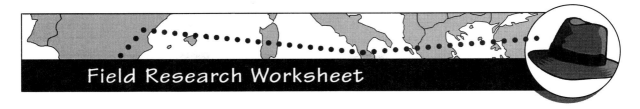

Field Research Worksheet

Now that you've learned a little about what a major in biology is like, think about what it means for you. Could this be a good choice for you? Can you say with reasonable certainty that it's not a good fit at all? Use the following planning worksheet to explain your response.

NO WAY!

Here are three reasons why I don't think this major would be a good choice for me.

_____

_____

_____

Stop! If you are sure this is not a major you want to pursue, don't waste another minute! Move on and explore another major.

A DEFINITE MAYBE

Here are three reasons why I think this major might be a good choice for me.

_____

_____

_____

Following are my plans to find out all I can about this major.

FIELD RESEARCH PROJECT 1: TALK ABOUT IT

I will use the materials in the Field Research section of this book (Part 5) to conduct interviews with the following people:

_____ Senior completing a major in biology

_____ Biology professor

_____ Biology professional

FIELD RESEARCH PROJECT 2: READ ABOUT IT

I will use Part 5 of this book to review the following book(s) about potential career tracks:

_____

_____

FIELD RESEARCH PROJECT 3: EXPERIENCE IT

I have arranged a tour or job-shadowing experience at the following location and will use Part 5 of this book to record my observations:

_____ Location

_____ Contact Person

_____ Date and Time of Appointment

FIELD RESEARCH PROJECT 4: EXPLORE THE OPTIONS

I want to find out all I can about the following career(s) and will use Part 5 of this book to guide my investigation at the library and on the Internet:

_____ Career Choice #1

_____ Career Choice #2

....

_____

Student's Name and Date

_____ Field Research Plan Approved

_____ Field Research Plan Not Approved

Because:

_____

_____

_____

Instructor's Signature and Date

....

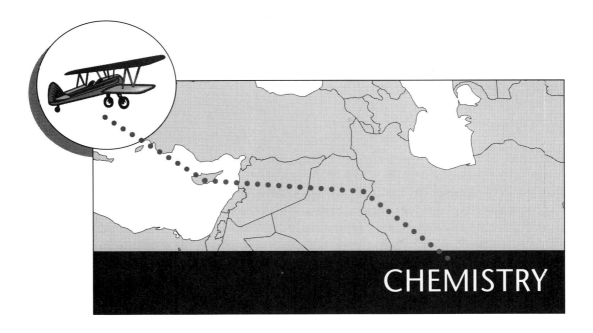

CHEMISTRY

Is This Major for You?

- Have you been concocting new formulas from the time you received your very first chemistry set as a child?
- Is the periodic table of elements as familiar to you as the back of your hand?
- Can you see yourself spending 60% of your work time in a lab or analyzing data with complex computer systems (as a high percentage of chemists indicate that they do)?
- Do you work well on a team?
- Do you get a kick out of trying to determine which ingredients various everyday products are made of?
- Are you curious and open-minded about facing new situations and problems?
- Do you like to think about the future and how life might differ from how it is now?

If you answered yes to several of these questions, keep reading and find out if a major in chemistry is a good choice for you.

INTRODUCTION

The shovel you left outside rusts and turns brownish-red. The wood in your fireplace burns and turns into ashes. The food you ate for lunch converted into energy (and other things) in your body, while plants convert sunlight and fertilizer into energy as well. Have you ever wondered how they figure out how many

Dr. Faye Rubinson, Chemistry Professor at the University of Cincinnati, contributed to this article.

grams of fat are in a fast-food hamburger, or if a vitamin pill really does contain 100% of your daily requirement of Vitamin B_6? Chemists seek to understand these elements and the processes they undergo to create the world around us. They analyze the nature of the elements with which we live.

WHAT IS CHEMISTRY?

Chemistry is the study of substances. Chemists study the composition of substances, how the substances act, and how they change. With this knowledge, they then try to determine why substances change and how they can be controlled. Everything is made up of chemical elements, which are tiny bits of matter called atoms, and each element's atoms are unique to it. When atoms of different elements combine, they form molecules of a chemical compound, the properties of which can be entirely different from each element alone. For example, take common salt, a safe compound that we use to season our food. It is composed of sodium, a soft, silvery-white metal, and chlorine, a poisonous, yellow-green gas. Separately, sodium and chlorine are not attractive—one of them is downright dangerous—but when chemically combined, they form a substance that is essential to human life.

HISTORY AND BACKGROUND

Humans have always experimented with the substances in their world to enhance their lives and create the things they need. Early Egyptian craftspeople made weapons, tools, and ornaments from copper, silver, and gold. They made bronze by melting tin and copper together. By experimentation, they learned to make glass, perfume, and wine, by combining different substances. Early Chinese and Greek philosophers developed theories about the substances in nature. They believed that all matter was derived from earth, fire, water, and air.

The earliest chemists were alchemists, searching for ways to turn substances into gold. Beginning about 300 B.C. and continuing through the 1600s, alchemy combined science, religion, philosophy, and magic. Alchemists improved on metal-making techniques, discovered many forms of acid, and developed early laboratory instruments and equipment. During the 1500s, alchemists and physicians began to combine their efforts and knowledge of chemistry to treat disease. This proved to be a turning point for chemistry. Since the time of the ancients, people had prepared and used drugs, but they didn't know why the drugs were effective. Now they became interested in chemical effects of medicines on the body. Another significant break from alchemy occurred in 1661, when Irish alchemist Robert Boyle used early scientific experimentation to support his theory that matter was made of atoms, and that earth, fire, water, and air were not elements.

By 1800, chemistry took another leap forward with the discovery of oxygen. The acceptance of oxygen as the essential element for sustaining life, present in air and the catalyst for many chemical reactions involving gases, was the beginning of modern chemistry. The field of chemistry grew during the 1800s with the discovery of half of the more than one hundred known elements. Because of the many areas of chemical inquiry, the field is now divided into four main branches—inorganic, organic, physical, and analytical.

INORGANIC CHEMISTRY. Study of compounds that do not contain carbon

ORGANIC CHEMISTRY. Study of compounds that contain carbon

Both organic and inorganic approaches are applied to geochemistry, polymer chemistry, synthetic chemistry, and colloid chemistry.

PHYSICAL CHEMISTRY. Uses mathematics to link physics and chemistry, and seeks to explain why chemical and physical processes take place; includes the study of thermodynamics, kinetics, quantum mechanics, spectroscopy, and statistical mechanics

ANALYTICAL CHEMISTRY. Analyzes what and how much chemical substance is present in a material in order to confirm its composition

Another area of chemistry that is now considered a part of biology is biochemistry. This is the study of chemical processes in living things. It is applied to medical chemistry and chemotherapy, molecular biophysics, pathological chemistry, and biogeochemistry. It is a discipline often studied for a career in the medical professions.

WHAT COURSES DO YOU NEED TO TAKE?

Though there are a number of specific areas on which to concentrate in postgraduate study, a bachelor's degree in chemistry includes courses in every aspect of the field.

Analytical Chemistry and Lab	General Physics and Lab
Analytical Geometry	Instrumental Analysis
Biochemistry	Organic Chemistry and Lab
Calculus	Physical Chemistry and Lab
General Chemistry and Lab	Physics

For a biochemistry emphasis, the following courses are generally required:

Biology	General Genetics
Cell Biology	Human Physiology
General Biochemistry and Lab	Microbiology

WHAT CAN YOU DO WITH A DEGREE IN CHEMISTRY?

A two-year degree allows you to work as a technician while finishing a bachelor's degree if you decide to go on. A bachelor's degree opens doors to careers in environmental analysis and science, the pharmaceutical industry, the petroleum industry, sales and manufacturing, and research and development. Jobs include air-pollution analyst, museum curator, criminologist, crime-lab analyst, public health educator, safety manager, sanitarian, soil scientist, water quality analyst, and technical/scientific writer. Advanced degrees prepare you for research in government and academic labs, or for teaching at the college level. A chemistry major is an excellent foundation for any medical profession.

BEFORE YOU DECIDE . . .

Before you invest the next four years pursuing this field of study, invest a few hours in a thorough investigation of what a degree in chemistry can do for you. Use the following suggestions and the worksheet at the end of this chapter to make a plan for conducting some field research. Once your plan is complete and approved by your instructor, proceed to Part 5, Field Research, where you'll find further instructions for making the most of these activities.

TALK ABOUT IT

Conduct interviews with the following three people (using the information included in the Field Research section in Part 5 of this book to guide your discussions):

- A senior completing a major in chemistry
- A chemistry professor at your school
- A professional working in a chemistry-related career

READ ABOUT IT

Following is a book listing that provides an overview of possible career options for someone with a degree in chemistry.

- Goldberg, Jan. *Real People Working in Science.* Lincolnwood, IL: VGM Career Horizons, 1998.
- *Job Choices in Science and Technology.* Bethlehem, PA: National Association of Colleges and Employers, 1998.
- Morgan, Bradley J. and Joseph M. Palmisano, eds. *Physical Sciences Career Directory.* Detroit: Visible Ink Press, 1994.
- Owens, Fred. *Careers for Chemists: A World Outside the Lab.* Washington, D. C.: American Chemical Society, 1996.
- Steiner, Peter D. *Discovering New Medicines: Careers in Pharmaceutical Research and Development.* New York: John Wiley & Sons, 1995.
- Woodburn, John H. *Opportunities in Chemistry Careers.* Lincolnwood, IL: VGM Career Horizons, 1996.

EXPERIENCE IT

Seek out an opportunity to see what a degree in chemistry can do for you in the workplace. Arrange a tour, a job-shadowing experience, or even a full-fledged internship at a place such as:

- A waste water treatment facility
- A pharmaceutical research laboratory
- A military chemical depot
- A cosmetic or perfume manufacturing plant
- A police crime lab (county, state, or national level)

Once you have scheduled a first appointment, use the information included in the Field Research section of this book to make the most of this experience.

EXPLORE THE OPTIONS

Here are some ways to put a degree in chemistry to work. Use this list for ideas but feel free to focus your exploration on another idea that interests you.

- Chemist
- Chemical Engineer
- Clinical Chemist
- Crime Lab Analyst
- Criminologist
- Environmental Engineer
- Industrial Chemist
- Lab Manager
- Medical Technologist
- Pharmaceutical Researcher
- Public Health Specialist
- Polymer Scientist
- Researcher
- Sanitarian
- Soil Scientist
- Technical Salesperson
- Technician
- Technical Writer

REFERENCES

Bruice, Paula. *Organic Chemistry.* Upper Saddle River, NJ: Prentice Hall, 1997.

McHale, Jeanne. *Molecular Spectroscopy.* Upper Saddle River, NJ: Prentice Hall, 1998.

Rubinson, Faye. *Contemporary Chemical Analysis.* Upper Saddle River, NJ: Prentice Hall, 1998.

Now that you've learned a little about what a major in chemistry is like, think about what it means for you. Could this be a good choice for you? Can you say with reasonable certainty that it's not a good fit at all? Use the following planning worksheet to explain your response.

NO WAY!

Here are three reasons why I don't think this major would be a good choice for me.

_____

_____

_____

Stop! If you are sure this is not a major you want to pursue, don't waste another minute! Move on and explore another major.

A DEFINITE MAYBE

Here are three reasons why I think this major might be a good choice for me.

_____

_____

_____

Following are my plans to find out all I can about this major.

FIELD RESEARCH PROJECT 1: TALK ABOUT IT

I will use the materials in the Field Research section of this book (Part 5) to conduct interviews with the following people:

_____ Senior completing a major in chemistry

_____ Chemistry professor

_____ Chemistry professional

FIELD RESEARCH PROJECT 2: READ ABOUT IT

I will use Part 5 of this book to review the following book(s) about potential career tracks.

_____

_____

Field Research Worksheet

FIELD RESEARCH PROJECT 3: EXPERIENCE IT

I have arranged a tour or job-shadowing experience at the following location and will use Part 5 of this book to record my observations.

_____ Location

_____ Contact Person

_____ Date and Time of Appointment

FIELD RESEARCH PROJECT 4: EXPLORE THE OPTIONS

I want to find out all I can about the following career(s) and will use Part 5 of this book to guide my investigation at the library and on the Internet:

_____ Career Choice #1

_____ Career Choice #2

....

_____

Student's Name and Date

_____ Field Research Plan Approved
_____ Field Research Plan Not Approved

Because:

_____

_____

_____

Instructor's Signature and Date

....

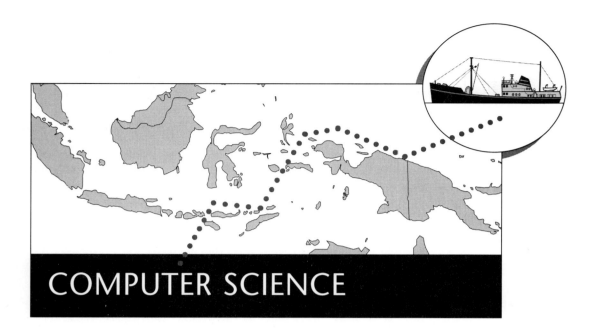

COMPUTER SCIENCE

Is This Major for You?

- Have you basically been hooked on computers from the very first time you used one?
- Do you tend to spend as much time as possible with your computer?
- Do you have a logical, orderly approach to problem-solving?
- Would you say that your interests are well-rounded (you have at least a little interest in a lot of areas) and that you would be comfortable applying your computer expertise in any number of environments?
- Does your curiosity about computers extend beyond a knowledge of what they can do to include a desire to know why and how they do what they do?
- Have you ever written a computer program (even if it is a simple one)?
- Do other people come to you when they have computer questions?
- Are you able to explain how to perform various tasks with computers in a way that other people can understand?
- Do you enjoy playing games and experimenting with new computer programs?
- Are you able to understand, organize, and tolerate the many painstaking steps it can take to complete a complex task?

If you answered yes to several of these questions, keep reading to find out if a computer science major is a good choice for you.

INTRODUCTION

Computers are present in nearly every aspect of our lives. We use personal computers at home and at work to perform tasks that are immediately necessary for

Dr. Joel Adams, Computer Science Professor at Calvin College, contributed to this article.

our daily personal and work requirements. Most of us are aware that computers are used for everything from sending email to controlling nuclear power. If solving problems with computer technology is fascinating to you, computer science may be the field you are looking for.

WHAT IS COMPUTER SCIENCE?

Computer science is the science of computation and, as such, it has two roots. The first is mathematical and deals with creating theoretical models. The second is an engineering root, which deals with implementation, both in the sense of hardware and in the structure of software. The science aspect of the field applies to finding boundaries and limitations of the content, speed, and efficiency of what can be computed. Computer science includes the study of algorithms, the step-by-step description of how to solve a problem. Algorithms then become the blueprints for problem solutions in the form of computer programs.

HISTORY AND BACKGROUND

Ancient Greeks used mathematics to solve problems, and the idea of algorithms (named in A.D. 825 for an Arabic mathematician) has been used for thousands of years. Where computations were done by the mind alone, now the computer is a tool to accomplish in seconds what once took hours, days, or even years.

There may be a number of algorithmic solutions to the same problem; one area of computer science is to determine the one that is most efficient. Scientists have learned much about problem-solving over the years. By the 1930s, they had determined that some problems would never be solvable even with today's computer technology. On the other hand, there are solvable problems that would take the foreseeable lifetime of the universe to solve. Then again, there are problems that computers can solve very efficiently.

So, what kinds of problems can be solved? If your "problem" is baking a cake, the recipe—the step-by-step instructions—solves it. If your problem is getting to school or work, the procedure you follow each morning to wake up, rise, and prepare yourself is the algorithm for that problem. On a more complicated level, encrypting and decrypting messages sent over the Internet is a problem that computers are used to solve. Computer science asks what the boundaries and limitations are for problem solving, and what real-world constraints must be considered in the solution.

COMPUTER SCIENCE TODAY

Computer scientists today are the problem-solvers of our high-tech society. Businesses use computer science problem-solving to address their needs. For example, Walmart wanted a more efficient inventory information system. They wanted to track sales and ship replacement items so they would not have too much or too little inventory on hand, therefore tying up as little of the cash flow as possible. With the solution they implemented, their business is run more efficiently, and they are doing well in a highly competitive industry.

Businesses use computer scientists to work in forecasting, analyze trends, and determine the direction of the future in areas like communications. Computer scientists maintain the infrastructure of communication networks such as the Internet. In addition, computer scientists work in programming, data base administration, systems analysis, and software engineering. Technology is here to stay, and the future is bright for computer science!

WHAT COURSES DO YOU NEED TO TAKE?

Basic courses in a computer science program include:

Algorithms	Introduction to Programming
Computer Organization	Operations Systems
Data Structures	Programming Languages
Discreet Mathematics	Statistics
Introduction to Hardware	

Electives include:

Artificial Intelligence	Human Computer Interfaces
Automata Theory	Multimedia
Compiler Construction	Networking
Computer Architecture	Software Engineering
Computer Graphics	Theory of Computation
Database Management	

In addition to course work, internship programs are an excellent way to gain experience in the field.

WHAT CAN YOU DO WITH A DEGREE IN COMPUTER SCIENCE?

The future is bright for computer scientists, especially those who complement their technical knowledge with communication and business skills. In addition to technical positions like technical administrator and software engineer, there are nontechnical career opportunities in product support, sales and marketing for wholesale and retail trade, documentation, and technical writing and editing. The demand for computer science majors is great, to the degree that industry recruiters are talking with qualified sophomore and junior undergraduates before they complete their degrees.

An advanced degree qualifies a computer scientist to work in a research lab or for a consulting firm. It qualifies her to teach at the college and university level, as well.

WHAT DO EXPERTS SAY ABOUT COMPUTER SCIENCE?

Dr. Joel Adams, Computer Science Professor at Calvin College, offers this advice to prospective students:

What can a person expect during this course of study? The course of study in the field of computer science involves highly technical study, but should be balanced with the liberal arts electives that will give a student in this discipline a well-rounded background. Regardless of how technically knowledgeable a person may be, too little knowledge of "softer" skills—communication, writing, business—is a disadvantage. Take courses that require group projects and presentations in order to acquire the interactive skills necessary to be successful in a career.

What are the characteristics of a successful student? The successful student in computer science enjoys problem solving. He has the tenacity to stick with it, an unwillingness to let a problem beat him. He must also pay attention to detail.

What do you see for the future of the discipline? The future is bright, especially for the well-rounded student who can function technically as well as interactively with associates.

What makes this field exciting to you, personally, and why do you love what you do? This field is exciting because it changes constantly from week to week, month to month. Courses that students took five years ago do not exist today and will not exist five years, or maybe even one year, from now. A person in this discipline definitely needs to be a lifelong learner, to keep reading and attending workshops and classes to stay current with all that is happening. People who don't keep up are called dinosaurs—you can imagine what happens to them. They become extinct!

BEFORE YOU DECIDE . . .

Before you invest the next four years pursuing this field of study, invest a few hours in a thorough investigation of what a degree in computer science can do for you. Use the following suggestions and the worksheet at the end of this chapter to make a plan for conducting some field research. Once your plan is complete and approved by your instructor, proceed to Part 5, Field Research, where you'll find further instructions for making the most of these activities.

TALK ABOUT IT

Conduct interviews with the following three people (using the information in the Field Research section in Part 5 to guide your discussions):

- A senior completing a major in computer science
- A computer science professor at your school
- A professional working in a computer-related career

READ ABOUT IT

Following is a book listing that provides an overview of possible career options for someone with a degree in computer science.

- Eberts, Marjorie and Margaret Gisler. *Careers for Computer Buffs and Other Technological Types.* Lincolnwood, IL: VGM Career Horizons, 1996.
- Eberts, Marjorie and Rachel Kelsey. *Careers for Cybersurfers and Other Online Types.* Lincolnwood, IL: VGM Career Horizons, 1998.
- Goldberg, Jan. *Great Jobs for Computer Science Majors.* Lincolnwood, IL: VGM Career Horizons, 1998.
- Hawkins, Lori and Betsy Dowling. *100 Jobs in Technology.* New York: Macmillan, 1996.
- Kling, Julie. *Opportunities in Computer Science Careers.* Lincolnwood, IL: VGM Career Horizons, 1991.
- Morgan, Bradley J. and Joseph M. Palmisani. *Computer and Software Design Career Directory.* Detroit: Gale Research Inc., 1993.
- Richardson, Peter and Bob Richardson. *Great Careers for People Interested in Math and Computers.* Detroit: Gale Reseach Inc., 1993.
- Schmidt, Peggy. *Career Choices for the 90's: Computer Science.* New York: Walker, 1990.
- Yanuck, Deborah and Gary Golter. *Opportunities in High Tech Careers.* Lincolnwood, IL: VGM Career Horizons, 1995.

EXPERIENCE IT

Seek out an opportunity to see what a degree in computer science can do for you in the workplace. Arrange a tour, a job-shadowing experience, or even a full-fledged internship at a place such as:

- Information systems department of a major corporation
- Computer component manufacturing firm
- Software design firm
- Computer equipment superstore
- Computer-related websites

Once you have scheduled a first appointment, use the information included in the Field Research section to make the most of this experience.

EXPLORE THE OPTIONS

Using the materials included in the Field Research section, conduct a thorough investigation of at least two career options for college graduates with a computer science degree. You'll need a good selection of career books and resources and access to the Internet to complete this task.

Here are some ways to put a degree in computer science to work. Use this list for ideas but feel free to focus your exploration on another idea that interests you.

- Artificial Intelligence Specialist
- College Professor
- Computer Consultant
- Computer Engineer
- Computer Programmer
- Demographer
- Electrical Engineer
- Equipment Salesperson
- Industrial Engineer
- Information Broker
- Information Specialist
- Internet Systems Administrator
- Manufacturer Engineer
- Multi-Media Program Designer
- Operations Manager
- Robotics Engineer
- Software Engineer
- Statistician
- Systems Analyst
- Teacher (K–12)
- Technical Support Specialist
- Technical Writer
- Trainer
- Webmaster

REFERENCE

Adams, Larry, Sanford Leestma, and Larry Nyhoff. *An Introduction to Computing.* Upper Saddle River, NJ: Prentice Hall, 1997.

Now that you've learned a little about what a major in computer science is like, think about what it means for you. Could this be a good choice for you? Can you say with reasonable certainty that it's not a good fit at all? Use the following planning worksheet to explain your response.

NO WAY!

Here are three reasons why I don't think this major would be a good choice for me.

_____

_____

_____

Stop! If you are sure this is not a major you want to pursue, don't waste another minute! Move on and explore another major.

A DEFINITE MAYBE

Here are three reasons why I think this major might be a good choice for me.

_____

_____

_____

Following are my plans to find out all I can about this major.

FIELD RESEARCH PROJECT 1: TALK ABOUT IT

I will use the materials in the Field Research section of this book (Part 5) to conduct interviews with the following people:

_____ Senior completing a major in computer science

_____ Computer science professor

_____ Computer science professional

FIELD RESEARCH PROJECT 2: READ ABOUT IT

I will use Part 5 of this book to review the following book(s) about potential career tracks:

_____

_____

FIELD RESEARCH PROJECT 3: EXPERIENCE IT

I have arranged a tour or job-shadowing experience at the following location and will use Part 5 of this book to record my observations:

_____ Location

_____ Contact Person

_____ Date and Time of Appointment

FIELD RESEARCH PROJECT 4: EXPLORE THE OPTIONS

I want to find out all I can about the following career(s) and will use Part 5 of this book to guide my investigation at the library and on the Internet:

_____ Career Choice #1

_____ Career Choice #2

· ·

_____

Student's Name and Date

_____ Field Research Plan Approved

_____ Field Research Plan Not Approved

Because:

_____

_____

_____

Instructor's Signature and Date

· ·

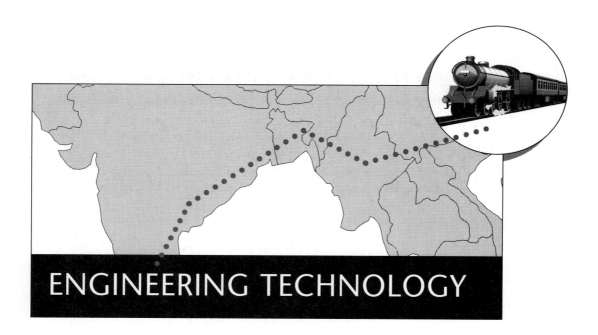

ENGINEERING TECHNOLOGY

Is This Major for You?

- Does it seem like you've always been curious about how things work?
- Do you tend to enjoy fixing things or just taking them apart and putting them together again just to see how they work?
- Are you logical, well-organized, and a good problem-solver?
- Does the prospect of working on huge, multimillion-dollar projects using the latest and greatest technology excite you?

If you answered yes to several of these questions, keep reading to find out if an engineering technology major is a good choice for you.

INTRODUCTION

Have you ever marveled at the pyramids of Egypt and of Central and South America? They were constructed with much trial and error and the labor of many people. But many of them are oriented with great accuracy to the movement of the sun or to cardinal points on the compass. Such accurate positioning required the use of a well-developed system of mathematics and science. These huge constructions helped humankind establish identity and satisfied the basic need to build and create. Engineering and technology activities satisfy this same basic need today. The early builders were the forerunners of today's civil, mechanical, and mining engineers.

Dr. Robert Pond, Engineering Technology Professor at Central Ohio Technical College, contributed to this article.

WHAT IS ENGINEERING TECHNOLOGY?

Engineering technologists are responsible for providing materials necessary for human subsistence and comfort. The world of technology is an ever-changing one, today even more than in the past. Technologists have the scientific, mathematical, and communication skills as well as the flexibility to confront the challenges presented by technological change. Transportation systems, buildings in which we live and work, automated industrial and business processes, improved power systems, new materials, more powerful computers, and highly integrated communication systems are some of the commodities provided by engineering technology.

HISTORY AND BACKGROUND

Modern engineering and technology began in the 1700s and developed into five main branches.

CIVIL ENGINEERING. Deals with the infrastructure or foundation; includes public utility systems, buildings, roads, railways, airports, bridges, and waterways

MECHANICAL ENGINEERING. Deals with the development of machine tooling and manufacturing

MINING AND METALLURGICAL ENGINEERING. Deals with how to mine minerals safely and efficiently, and how to improve metallic properties

CHEMICAL ENGINEERING. Deals with controlling chemical processes that convert raw materials into useful commodities

ELECTRICAL ENGINEERING. Youngest, yet largest branch of engineering, concerned with production and distribution of electrical energy (power plants and power lines)

ENGINEERING TECHNOLOGY TODAY

Industry requires teamwork of the scientist, engineer, technician, technologist, and skilled worker. The scientist engages in research and development of new materials; the engineer provides system design and technical support. The technician and technologist provide the practical, hands-on manufacturing expertise. The skilled worker operates and repairs specialized machinery. Today, demand has created over thirty different engineering fields from the original five main branches. Some of these new degree areas are:

- Aerospace
- Agricultural
- Architectural
- Biomedical
- Computer
- Electromechanical
- Engineering science

- Environmental
- Industrial Systems
- Marine Welding
- Materials
- Nuclear
- Petroleum

Technicians and technologists work in key positions on the manufacturing team. People with two-year (technicians) and four-year (technologist) degrees work today as

COMMUNICATORS. Providing clear communication between engineer and skilled worker

IMPLEMENTORS. Interpreting and implementing the ideas of the engineer

CALIBRATORS AND TESTERS. Performing complicated tests in engineering laboratories

MANUFACTURING ENGINEERS. Supervising skilled and semiskilled personnel and solving problems in manufacturing processes

WHAT COURSES DO YOU NEED TO TAKE?

Electives that will enhance marketability in engineering technology, in addition to technical courses, include courses in psychology, sociology, communications (public speaking and writing), ethics, and international relations. Requirements include:

- Algebra
- Calculus
- Circuits
- Computers for Engineering
- Digital Electronics
- Drafting
- Electronic Manufacturing Processes
- Fluid Power Control
- Hydraulics and Pneumatics
- Industrial Electronics
- Instrumentation and Control
- Physics–Mechanics
- Physics of Heat, Light, and Sound
- Trigonometry

WHAT CAN YOU DO WITH A DEGREE IN ENGINEERING TECHNOLOGY?

The future is bright for engineering technology. An increasing need for automation in all areas of government and business assures a demand for qualified technical people. National, state, and city governments hire health and regulatory inspectors to enforce the wide range of regulations to protect public health and safety. Major areas of employment are:

Chemical Engineering Technician
Civil and Architectural Engineering Technician
Computer Engineering Technician
Electrical/Electronic Engineering Technician
Industrial Engineering Technician
Mechanical Engineering Technician

An engineering technician is expected to learn her job quickly. Because she is prepared for hands-on applications as well as theoretical applications, an employer expects her to learn a new process or to perform a new lab test as the need arises.

ADVICE FROM THE EXPERTS

Dr. Robert Pond, Engineering Technology Professor at Central Ohio Technical College, offers this advice to prospective students:

What can a person expect during the course of study in this discipline? Most engineering tech students enroll in a two-year associate degree program, which may lead to a four-year program in engineering. Courses in communications, mathematics, and science focus on applications. In addition, a student can expect to work on a team. He should plan to be in class or doing homework at least 40 hours a week. When considering this field, realize what is expected of the successful technician.

- a strong work ethic and knowledge of engineering principles
- good report-writing skills coupled with competency in oral communications
- the ability to work well with others
- a thorough understanding of computers and of computer-integrated manufacturing
- a variety of basic Industrial Engineering Technology (IET) skills (costing, pricing, material selection)
- a variety of mechanical engineering technology skills

What are the characteristics of a successful student in this discipline? A successful student has the ability to read and write; she must listen and speak well to be effective as a team member; she has a strong interest in applied math and science; and she is adept in the use of computers. She is curious about electronic and mechanical systems and how they interrelate.

What are future opportunities in the field? The future is bright with opportunities in many fields. Technology is driving our economy now and will continue to do so in developing countries. There will be many more jobs in the field. People will occupy leadership positions in industry.

What makes you passionate about your field? Why did you choose it? I feel passionate about this area because I like the challenges of an ever-changing environment and the many problem-solving opportunities. There is constant change in this field; not everyone likes this, but I do. I can be more competitive if I keep up with the changes and welcome them. This field is about implementation—taking the findings of scientists and engineers and bringing them to reality.

BEFORE YOU DECIDE . . .

Before you invest the next four years pursuing this field of study, invest a few hours in a thorough investigation of what a degree in engineering technology can do for you. Use the following suggestions and the worksheet at the end of this chapter to make a plan for conducting some field research. Once your plan is complete and approved by your instructor, proceed to Part 5, Field Research, where you'll find further instructions for making the most of these activities.

TALK ABOUT IT

Conduct interviews with the following three people (using the information included in the Field Research section in Part 5 of this book to guide your discussions):

- A senior completing a major in engineering
- An engineering professor at your school
- A professional working in an engineering-related career

READ ABOUT IT

Following is a book listing that provides an overview of possible career options for someone with a degree in engineering technology.

- Basta, Nicolas. *Careers in High Tech.* Lincolnwood, IL: NTC Publishing, 1992.
- *Careers in Science and Engineering: An International Perspective.* Washington, D. C.: National Academy Press, 1996.
- Garner, Geraldine O. *Careers in Engineering.* Lincolnwood, IL: VGM Career Horizons, 1993.
- Hawkins, Lori and Betsy Dowling. *100 Jobs in Technology.* New York: Macmillan, 1997.
- Hoschette, John A. *Career Advancement and Survival for Engineers.* NY: John Wiley & Sons, 1994.
- *Job Choices in Science and Engineering.* Bethlehem, PA: National Association of Colleges and Employers, 1998.
- Rosen, Stephen and Cecilia Paul. *Career Renewal. Tools for Science and Technology Professionals.* Orlando, FL: Academic Press, 1997.
- Walsh, Stuart G. *Engineering Your Future. Launching a Successful Entry Level Technical Career in Today's Business Environment.* Upper Saddle River, NJ: Prentice Hall, 1995.

EXPERIENCE IT

Seek out an opportunity to see what a degree in engineering technology can do for you in the workplace. Arrange a tour, a job-shadowing experience, or even a full-fledged internship at a place such as:

- A manufacturing plant
- A major construction site
- An architectural firm
- A large farming cooperative
- An engineering firm
- An Army Corps of Engineers battalion
- An airplane maintenance hangar or manufacturing plant
- An automotive design center

Once you have scheduled a first appointment, use the information included in the Field Research section of this book to make the most of this experience.

EXPLORE THE OPTIONS

Using the materials included in the Field Research section at the end of this book, conduct a thorough investigation of at least two career options for college graduates with an engineering technology degree. You'll need a good selection of career books and resources and access to the Internet to complete this task. Here are some ways to put a degree in engineering technology to work. Use this list for ideas but feel free to focus your exploration on another idea that interests you.

- Aerospace Engineer
- Agricultural Engineer
- Architectural Engineer
- Artificial Intelligence Specialist
- Automotive Engineer
- Ceramic Engineer
- Computer Engineer
- Electrical Engineer
- Environmental Engineer
- Fire Protection Engineer
- Geological Engineer
- Geothermal Engineer
- Heating, Ventilator, and Refrigeration Engineer
- Industrial Engineer
- Manufacturing Engineer
- Materials Engineer
- Mechanical Engineer
- Metallurgical Engineer
- Mining Engineer
- Naval Engineer
- Nuclear Engineer
- Oceanic Engineer
- Petroleum Engineer
- Robotics Engineer
- Safety Engineer
- Software Engineer
- Transportation Engineer

REFERENCE

Pond, Robert J. *Introduction to Engineering Technology.* Upper Saddle River, NJ: Prentice Hall, 1996.

Now that you've learned a little about what a major in engineering technology is like, think about what it means for you. Could this be a good choice? Can you say with reasonable certainty that it's not a good fit at all? Use the following planning worksheet to explain your response.

NO WAY!

Here are three reasons why I don't think this major would be a good choice for me.

_____

_____

_____

Stop! If you are sure this is not a major you want to pursue, don't waste another minute! Move on and explore another major.

A DEFINITE MAYBE

Here are three reasons why I think this major might be a good choice for me.

_____

_____

_____

Following are my plans to find out all I can about this major.

FIELD RESEARCH PROJECT 1: TALK ABOUT IT

I will use materials included in the Field Research section of this book (Part 5) to conduct interviews with the following people:

_____ Senior completing a major in engineering technology

_____ Engineering technology professor

_____ Engineering technology professional

FIELD RESEARCH PROJECT 2: READ ABOUT T

I will use the materials included in Part 5 of this book to review the following book(s) about potential career tracks:

_____

_____

Field Research Worksheet

FIELD RESEARCH PROJECT 3: EXPERIENCE IT

I have arranged a tour or job-shadowing experience at the following location and will use the materials included in Part 5 of this book to record my observations:

_____ Location

_____ Contact Person

_____ Date and Time of Appointment

FIELD RESEARCH PROJECT 4: EXPLORE THE OPTIONS

I want to find out all I can about the following career(s) and will use the materials included in Part 5 of this book to guide my investigation at the library and on the Internet:

_____ Career Choice #1

_____ Career Choice #2

....

_____

Student's Name and Date

_____ Field Research Plan Approved

_____ Field Research Plan Not Approved

Because:

_____

_____

_____

Instructor's Signature and Date

....

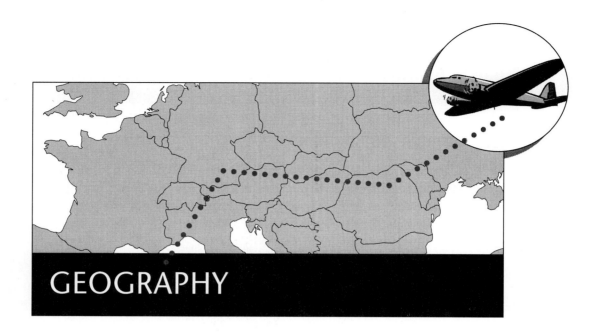

GEOGRAPHY

Is This Major for You?

- Can you imagine the important role that geography plays in world problems such as world hunger, environmental quality, water management, urban development, crime, transportation, and hazardous waste disposal?
- Are you interested in a field that has captivated the attention of the likes of basketball great Michael Jordan (a geography major at the University of North Carolina, Chapel Hill, before he made it big in basketball) and the late humanitarian Mother Teresa (who started her career as a geography teacher in Calcutta, India)?
- Do you have a better chance than most of finding your way from Point A to Point B via your map reading skills?
- Are you interested in learning the role that geography plays in world affairs?
- Can you imagine the role geographic dimensions might play in any number of society's problems and would you like to work toward finding solutions?

If you answered yes to several of these questions, keep reading to find out if a geography major is a good choice for you.

INTRODUCTION

Imagine that you just put down today's newspaper. You read that experts can't agree on whether or not Earth is warming, and if so, whether global warming is bad. You learn how the value of the Japanese yen and forest fires in Indonesia

Dr. Robert Christopherson, Geography Professor at American Renir College in Sacramento; Dr. David Clawson, Geography Professor at the University of New Orleans; and Dr. Jim Rubenstein, Geography Professor at Miami University in Oxford, Ohio, contributed to this article.

directly affect our economy and environment. You fear that a conflict among unfamiliar cultural groups in a far-away place can cut off our oil supplies and even require sending our troops abroad. Behind our understanding of these relationships is the fascinating field of geography.

WHAT IS GEOGRAPHY?

Geography is the study of where people and environments occur on Earth and the reasons for their location. It explores the interdependence among people and environment in different places. Geographers ask where things are and why they are there. Geography integrates knowledge from the social sciences and natural sciences.

Historians organize material by time whereas geographers organize material by place. Historians understand that past actions can affect future ones. Geographers understand that something happening at one place can be the effect of something that has happened elsewhere. Geography matters in the contemporary world because it can explain human actions and physical processes at all scales, from local to global. At a global scale, geographers understand reasons for population growth, climate change, political conflict, and increased pollution. At a personal scale, geographers can explain where you live, what route you take to work or class, and why trees in your backyard are dying.

Geography divides broadly into two categories—human geography and physical geography. Human geographers study why human activities are located where they are (for example, religions, businesses, and cities). Physical geographers study why natural forces occur as they do (for example, climates, land forms, and types of vegetation).

HISTORY AND BACKGROUND

The word *geography* comes from the Greek words *geo* (earth) and *graphein* (to describe or write about). The first geographer was the first unknown prehistoric human who crossed a river or climbed a hill, observed what was on the other side, returned home to tell about it, and scratched a rough map in the dirt to depict the route. Early humans used elementary knowledge of geography to determine the best ways to find food and shelter. The ancient Greeks were the first to demonstrate the practical importance of geographical knowledge. Greek philosophers realized that geography was the best way to understand the interdependence between people and nature and between different places. They applied their understanding to practical areas like business, trade, astronomy, map-making (known as cartography), as well as to philosophical aspects of understanding nature and society.

During the Age of Discovery, European explorers depended on geographers to prepare accurate maps of the known world and to write detailed descriptions of newly explored places. Around 1800, European scholars began to move geographical study away from straightforward descriptions of the Earth toward the explanation of interrelationships. Having largely completed the task of accurately mapping Earth, contemporary geographers apply new technologies to learn more about places. Two important mapping technologies developed during the past quarter-century: remote sensing from satellites to collect data, and geographic information systems, which are computer programs for handling geographic data and preparing maps.

GEOGRAPHY TODAY

Modern communications and technology have fostered globalization, pulling people into greater interaction with each other and with their environment. At the same time, people are searching for ways to express their unique traditions and preserve unique environments. Geographers study the tensions between two geographic trends, globalization versus local diversity, which underlie many of the world's problems.

Today humans are capable of altering the environment on a global scale through global warming, deforestation, acid rain deposition, soil erosion, and groundwater contamination. The effects of these changes on the world, now and in the future, concern geographers. A geography curriculum prepares someone to meet these challenges and find ways to solve the problems facing our planet.

WHAT COURSES DO YOU NEED TO TAKE?

Most universities and colleges require a core curriculum comprising liberal arts courses to provide an overall body of knowledge. Because Latin America is increasingly important in the global economy, geography students can enhance their employment prospects by learning Spanish. Computing skills are especially important for geographers because most maps are now made with computer software. Presentation, speaking, and writing skills are also highly recommended. Introductory courses for a major in geography include:

Economic Geography	Introduction to Physical Geography
Historical Geography	Introduction to World Regional
Introduction to Human or	Geography
Cultural Geography	Weather and Climate

Specialization in one or more major areas of geography is possible, depending on interests. Human geographers take courses in economic geography, urban geography, and urban planning. Physical geographers take courses in climatology, biogeography, and geomorphology. Regional geographers take courses in political geography, economic development, and specific regions, such as Latin America, East Asia, or the Middle East. In addition, geography students are expected to learn analytic tools of the trade, such as mapping principles, Geographic Information Systems (GIS), and statistics.

A student may also minor in geography. Refer to the continuum of fields embraced by geography. A minor in geography may be a useful complement to another major.

WHAT CAN YOU DO WITH A DEGREE IN GEOGRAPHY?

A degree in geography enables you to do two types of jobs. First, you can be an expert in a subfield of geography, such as economic geography, geomorphology, or GIS. Second, you can be a well-rounded generalist who contributes a broad perspective to a variety of problems. Regardless of whether you are a generalist or specialist geographer, jobs are available in government or private industry. Local, state, and federal government offices hire geographers to work in environmental protection, urban planning, economic development, parks and recreation, transportation, housing, data analysis, social services, and foreign service. You can work with private consultants, real estate developers, nonprofit agencies, banks, retailers, and companies doing business overseas.

Geography's future looks bright. Faced with the global crisis of diminishing natural resources and increasing population, humans are reassessing their relationship with the natural environment and reevaluating solutions for protecting our planet. Geographers have the knowledge and skills to help provide answers.

WHAT DO EXPERTS SAY ABOUT GEOGRAPHY?

Dr. Jim Rubenstein, Geography Professor at Miami University in Oxford, Ohio, offers this advice to prospective students:

What can a person expect during the course of study? Geography is partly a social science and partly a natural science. The student can expect to study both of these. She will also spend a lot of time analyzing maps and making maps on computers.

What are the characteristics of a successful student? A successful student is fascinated with the complexities of the world and wants to make the world safer and more attractive. A geography student cares about the environment or a particular place—either near or far—and loves to study and make maps. If you enjoy looking through an atlas and wonder about how everything fits together, then consider geography.

What do you see for the future of the discipline? The brightest future in geography is applying technical knowledge to understand problems of location. Geographers learn tools for analyzing the relationship of the location of a new shopping mall to the location of a contaminated stream. The ability to use GIS is in heavy demand.

Geography faces two fundamental challenges. First, scientists who don't understand the importance of location sometimes equate geography with glossy picture magazines. Second, jobs and careers in geography rarely carry the title "geographer."

What makes this field exciting to you, personally, and why do you love what you do? I love geography because I love maps. Maps jump off the page and speak eloquently to geographers. Geographers also love the ability to synthesize a wide variety of subjects from both the social and natural sciences. I chose geography as a career because I was always interested in cities. I wanted to make cities better places to live.

BEFORE YOU DECIDE . . .

Before you invest the next four years pursuing this field of study, invest a few hours in a thorough investigation of what a degree in geography can do for you. Use the following suggestions and the worksheet at the end of this chapter to make a plan for conducting some field research. Once your plan is complete and approved by your instructor, proceed to Part 5, Field Research, where you'll find further instructions for making the most of these activities.

TALK ABOUT IT

Conduct interviews with the following three people (using the information included in the Field Research section in Part 5 of this book to guide your discussions):

- A senior completing a major in geography
- A geography professor at your school
- A professional working in a geography-related career

READ ABOUT IT

Following is a book listing that provides an overview of possible career options for someone with a degree in geography.

- Boehm, Richard. *Careers in Geography.* Washington, D.C.: Association of American Geographers, 1996.
- *Geography: Today's Career for Tomorrow.* (You can order this booklet from the Association of American Geographers, 1710 Sixteenth Street, NW, Washington, D.C. 20009.)
- Roth, Richard. *What Can You Do With a Geography Degree?* Seattle, WA: University of Washington, Department of Geography.

EXPERIENCE IT

Seek out an opportunity to see what a degree in geography can do for you in the workplace. Arrange a tour, a job-shadowing experience, or even a full-fledged internship at a place such as:

- A real estate development company
- A national park's office
- A nonprofit environmental organization
- A government agency such as the Census Bureau or the U. S. Geological Survey
- A publisher of maps or other travel-related publications
- An airport control tower

Once you have scheduled a first appointment, use the information included in the Field Research section of this book to make the most of this experience.

EXPLORE THE OPTIONS

Using the materials included in the Field Research section at the end of this book, conduct a thorough investigation of at least two career options for college graduates with a geology degree. You'll need a good selection of career books and resources and access to the Internet to complete this task.

Here are some ways to put a degree in geology to work. Use this list for ideas but feel free to focus your exploration on another idea that interests you.

- Cartographer
- Census Geographer
- Climatologist
- College Professor
- Community Developer
- Conservationist
- Demographer
- Diplomat
- Environmental Manager
- Facility Planner

- Hydrologist
- Land Developer
- Land-Use Analyst
- Map Editor
- Market Analyst
- Real Estate Developer
- Teacher (K–12)
- Travel Specialist
- Urban Planner

REFERENCES

Christopherson, Robert. *Geosystems.* Upper Saddle River, NJ: Prentice Hall, 1997.

Clawson, David and James Fisher. *World Regional Geography: A Development Approach.* Upper Saddle River, NJ: Prentice Hall, 1998.

Rubenstein, James. *Introduction to Human Geography.* Upper Saddle River, NJ: Prentice Hall, 1996.

Now that you've learned a little about what a major in geology is like, think about what it means for you. Could this be a good choice for you? Can you say with reasonable certainty that it's not a good fit at all? Use the following planning worksheet to explain your response.

NO WAY!

Here are three reasons why I don't think this major would be a good choice for me.

_____

_____

_____

Stop! If you are sure this is not a major you want to pursue, don't waste another minute! Move on and explore another major.

A DEFINITE MAYBE

Here are three reasons why I think this major might be a good choice for me.

_____

_____

_____

Following are my plans to find out all I can about this major.

FIELD RESEARCH PROJECT 1: TALK ABOUT IT

I will use materials included in the Field Research section of this book (Part 5) to conduct interviews with the following people:

_____ Senior completing a major in geology

_____ Geology professor

_____ Geology professional

FIELD RESEARCH PROJECT 2: READ ABOUT IT

I will use the materials included in Part 5 of this book to review the following book(s) about potential career tracks:

_____

_____

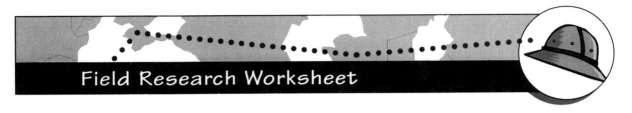

Field Research Worksheet

FIELD RESEARCH PROJECT 3: EXPERIENCE IT

I have arranged a tour or job-shadowing experience at the following location and will use the materials included in Part 5 of this book to record my observations:

_____ Location

_____ Contact Person

_____ Date and Time of Appointment

FIELD RESEARCH PROJECT 4: EXPLORE THE OPTIONS

I want to find out all I can about the following career(s) and will use the materials included in Part 5 of this book to guide my investigation at the library and on the Internet:

_____ Career Choice #1

_____ Career Choice #2

_____

Student's Name and Date

_____ Field Research Plan Approved

_____ Field Research Plan Not Approved

Because:

_____

_____

_____

Instructor's Signature and Date

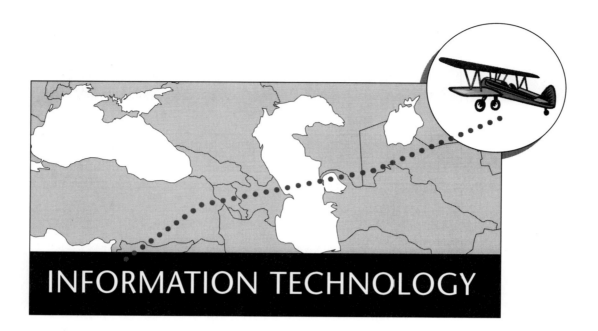

INFORMATION TECHNOLOGY

Is This Major for You?

- Do you have an appreciation for what the intelligent use of technology can do to further the success of businesses of all sizes?
- Are you willing to work in an environment where rapid change is the norm?
- Is your fascination with technology strong enough to sustain a life-long learning curve in order to keep up with new developments?
- Are you logical and well-organized in your approach to problem-solving?
- Does the idea of working with massive amounts of information and the most advanced technology appeal to you?
- Have you read about technology problems, such as the "year 2000 glitch," and wondered what you could do to fix them?
- Are you able to communicate complex information in such a way that others can understand?

If you answered yes to several of these questions, keep reading to find out if a major in information technology is a good choice for you.

INTRODUCTION

In the future, someone in the market for a new home will be able to visit any house for sale in the country from the comfort of her own home or office via computer. She will tell the computer what city to search, as well as other pertinent details. The electronic "real estate agent" will then list appropriate prospects, provide her with detailed information on the house and surrounding

Dr. Larry Long, Professor and Business Consultant with Long & Associates, contributed to this article.

area, and take her on a "tour" of the house, inside and out. After the house tour, she can "drive" through the neighborhood, looking left and right as she would from her car. Seem like a long way off? It's already happening—virtually all of California's real estate listings can be viewed on your computer. Systems that permit neighborhood drive-throughs are under active development! Welcome to one of the many applications of information technology!

WHAT IS INFORMATION TECHNOLOGY?

Information technology is the integration of information systems and computing technology. Computer-based information systems combine hardware, software, people, procedures, and data to provide people with data processing capabilities and information for the efficient operation of their lives. Information technology has an impact on nearly every aspect of our lives, at home, at work, and at play. From ATMs to video games to Internet research, we are all caught up in the use of information technology.

HISTORY AND BACKGROUND

Fifty years ago, there were no computers as we know them today. In the 1960s, mammoth multimillion-dollar computers processed data for large companies that could afford them. These machines were operated by highly specialized technicians who served as intermediaries between the people who used the computers and the computer system. In the 1970s, computers became smaller and more accessible, which led to the introduction of the personal computer. From that point to the present, millions of people from all walks of life have purchased PCs that have revolutionized the way they conduct their business and personal lives.

Today one in four Americans has a home computer more powerful than those that processed data for large companies during the 1960s! The widespread availability of computers has prompted an explosion of applications. At home, you can use your PC to go on a fantasy adventure or hold an electronic reunion with your scattered family. At the corporate level, virtually every business uses information technology (IT), the integration of computing technology and information processing, to offer better services and gain a competitive advantage.

INFORMATION TECHNOLOGY TODAY

The technological revolution, anchored by the computer, has changed the way we communicate, do business, and learn—and technology changes rapidly. We live in an information age, with the information superhighway (a network of high-speed data communications links, including the Internet) that connects virtually every facet of our society. Computer competency is essential today for success in business and education. At more than 3,000 colleges and universities, computer courses are becoming the only area of study, other than English, that is required. The advent of computer technology has also rendered a number of traditional college disciplines extinct or completely changed the way things are done. Drafting, for example, is now done by computer-aided design.

Most businesses have their own information technology departments, but even the smallest companies need information technology specialists, or knowledge workers. There are thousands of IT consulting companies that cater to the needs of all types of businesses. These independent consultants are literally how IT is supported, because it is not possible to predict the size and complexity of specific business needs: large companies may need additional help for a large project, and smaller businesses may not have the resources to hire knowledge workers but require their support just the same.

Technology is driving our society, and the future is difficult to predict. Information technology keeps our world together—a bank, for example, can only live thirty hours without its IT system before it can no longer function. A calendar year has twelve months, but an Internet year—the rate at which technology is changing—is only two months. For every one calendar year, technology is advancing *six years*. Business, communication, science and research, health care, education, and entertainment—all are part of the rapidly evolving world of information technology.

WHAT COURSES DO YOU NEED TO TAKE?

The speed at which IT has overtaken the world has found many students unprepared to meet educational demands. Too often, high school graduates arrive at college with too few science and math courses to be successful in the required computer and science curriculums. It cannot be overemphasized that you take all the courses you can in high school to prepare yourself for college-level technology study. Information technology is applicable to any field, and more colleges are offering discipline-specific courses. Realize that regardless of your field of interest—music, accounting, education—you can design a degree plan to integrate that interest with IT. The following are the types of requirements and electives generally available:

Introduction to Computer Information Systems
Business Information Systems
COBOL Implementation of Management Information Systems
Advanced COBOL and Production Application Systems
Current Topics in Computer Information Systems
Business Application Systems Development
Structural Systems Analysis
Information Systems Analysis
Decision Support Systems
End User Computing
Centralized Data Systems
Object-Oriented Technologies

WHAT CAN YOU DO WITH A DEGREE IN *IT?*

Information technology impacts every field, and there simply are not enough graduating students to accommodate the demand. In the United States alone, 350,000 jobs will go unfilled for lack of qualified technical graduates. There is literally a new career field being created every few months that did not exist in the past. For example, two years ago, web page designing was not a career field; now it is.

Information technology departments within corporations include positions as chief information officer (CIO), programmers and systems analysts, network designers and administrators, LANS (local area networks) specialists, Internet site specialists, and user liaisons (communication specialists who interface with the computer users). Other positions that may or may not require a degree are job and data specialists and PC specialists who work at help desks. Because many companies rely on outsourcing to supply their IT needs, there are thousands of consulting opportunities.

With the rapidly changing nature of the industry, continuing education in the private sector offers innumerable opportunities. Any employee who uses computing must continually be instructed as upgrades and new programs are installed. There are more instructors today in the corporate world than in colleges, and over half of them teach IT.

WHAT DO EXPERTS SAY ABOUT INFORMATION TECHNOLOGY?

Dr. Larry Long, Professor and Business Consultant, offers this advice to prospective students:

What can a person expect during the course of study? Students who come to college prepared will face many scientific and intellectual challenges. They will gather the tools that will help them do a variety of jobs. In almost any area of the business world, graduates are assured of jobs.

What are the characteristics of a successful student? The successful student is inquisitive and able to synthesize information. He is also able to work and interact well with people. More than other disciplines, technical people need interpersonal communication skills.

What do you see for the future of the discipline? The future is unknown—a new career field is created every year. Technology is driving our society at an incredible rate. We are not as prepared as countries like Russia, Japan, and Germany, who require high school equivalent students to learn more science and math so that they have more choices about what to pursue as they continue their education. We need to encourage our own students to take more challenging courses to prepare for the high-tech age.

What makes this field exciting to you, personally, and why do you love what you do? Having grown up with computers all of my working life, I feel like they are part of my being. My job as an author is to portray the field of IT as it really is—challenging, exciting, and full of opportunities, especially in online education.

BEFORE YOU DECIDE . . .

Before you invest the next four years pursuing this field of study, invest a few hours in a thorough investigation of what a degree in information technology can do for you. Use the following suggestions and the worksheet at the end of this chapter to make a plan for conducting some field research. Once your plan is complete and approved by your instructor, proceed to Part 5, Field Research, where you'll find further instructions for making the most of these activities.

TALK ABOUT IT

Conduct interviews with the following three people (using the information included in the Field Research section in Part 5 of this book to guide your discussions):

- A senior completing a degree in information technology
- An information technology professor at your school
- A professional working in an information technology career

READ ABOUT IT

Following is a book listing that provides an overview of possible career options for someone with a degree in information technology.

- Altman, Don B. *Digital Frontier Job and Opportunity Finder: Tomorrow's Opportunities Today.* Los Angeles: Moon Lake Media, 1996.
- Cosgrove, Holli R. *Exploring Technical Careers: Real People Tell You What You Need to Know.* Chicago: Ferguson, 1995.
- *Getting Technical* (Volumes 1–4). Minneapolis: Finney, 1997.
- Hawkins, Lori. *100 Jobs in Technology.* New York: Macmillan, 1996.
- Higman, Susan. *Jobs You Can Live With: Working At the Crossroads of Science, Technology, and Society.* Washington, D. C.: Student Pugman USA, 1996.
- Hunt, Christopher and Scott A. Scanlon. *Job Seeker's Guide to Silicon Valley Recruiters.* NY: John Wiley & Sons, 1998.
- McNeill, William P. *Job Bank Guide to Computer and High Tech Companies.* Holbrook, MA: Adams Media Corp., 1997.
- Spencer, Jean W. *Careers Inside the World of Technology.* New York: Rosen Publishing Group, 1995.
- Spivach, Jane F. *Careers in Information.* New York: Macmillan, 1982.

EXPERIENCE IT

Seek out an opportunity to see what a degree in information technology can do for you in the workplace. Arrange a tour, a job-shadowing experience, or even a full-fledged internship at a place such as:

- The information systems department of any corporation
- CD ROM publishing company
- A software development firm
- Headquarters for an Internet access provider
- Office of an independent computer consultant

Once you have scheduled a first appointment, use the information included in the Field Research section of this book to make the most of this experience.

EXPLORE THE OPTIONS

- CD-ROM Producer
- College Professor
- Computer Game Programmer
- Computer Integrated Manufacturing Manager
- Computer Programmer
- Electronics Technician
- Functional Analyst
- Internet Access Provider
- Local Area Network (LAN) Specialist
- Manager of Information Systems (MIS)

- Multimedia Producer
- Software Engineer
- Software Integration Engineer
- Software Tools Developer
- Systems Analyst
- Systems Architect
- Systems Engineer
- Technical Writer
- Website Designer
- Webmaster

REFERENCE

Long, Larry and Nancy Long. *Computers.* Upper Saddle River, NJ: Prentice Hall, 1997.

Now that you've learned a little about what a major in information technology is like, think about what it means for you. Could this be a good choice? Can you say with reasonable certainty that it's not a good fit at all? Use the following planning worksheet to explain your response.

NO WAY!

Here are three reasons why I don't think this major would be a good choice for me.

_____

_____

_____

Stop! If you are sure this is not a major you want to pursue, don't waste another minute! Move on and explore another major.

A DEFINITE MAYBE

Here are three reasons why I think this major might be a good choice for me.

_____

_____

_____

Following are my plans to find out all I can about this major.

FIELD RESEARCH PROJECT 1: TALK ABOUT IT

I will use materials included in the Field Research section of this book to conduct interviews with the following people:

_____ Senior completing a major in information technology

_____ Information technology professor

_____ Information technology professional

FIELD RESEARCH PROJECT 2: READ ABOUT IT

I will use the materials included in the Field Research section of this book (Part 5) to review the following book(s) about potential career tracks:

_____

_____

FIELD RESEARCH PROJECT 3: EXPERIENCE IT

I have arranged a tour or job-shadowing experience at the following location and will use the materials included in Part 5 of this book to record my observations:

_____ Location

_____ Contact Person

_____ Date and Time of Appointment

FIELD RESEARCH PROJECT 4: EXPLORE THE OPTIONS

I want to find out all I can about the following career(s) and will use the materials included in Part 5 of this book to guide my investigation at the library and on the Internet:

_____ Career Choice #1

_____ Career Choice #2

....

_____

Student's Name and Date

_____ Field Research Plan Approved

_____ Field Research Plan Not Approved

Because:

_____

_____

_____

Instructor's Signature and Date

....

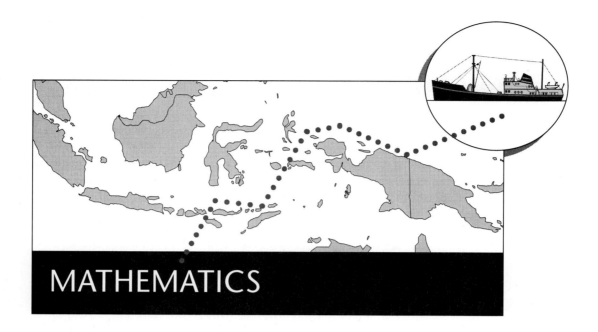

MATHEMATICS

Is This Major for You?

- Are you naturally curious about the world around you?
- Does the idea of approaching problem-solving with reasoning, intuition, and imagination appeal to you?
- Are you interested in entering a field where five math-based professions ranked in the top 10 of 244 rated by *Jobs Rated Almanac* (top math professions were actuary, software engineer, computer analyst, mathematician, and statistician)?
- Is it important to you that your earning potential be higher than average (according to a study conducted by the University of Michigan, the starting salary for graduates with a math major was $28,933 in 1996)?
- Do you enjoy math classes?
- Do you find the challenge of working through complex mathematical equations satisfying?
- Would you like numbers to play a big part in your future career?

If you answered yes to several of these questions, keep reading to find out if a major in mathematics is a good choice for you.

INTRODUCTION

It is through an understanding of mathematics that we understand and impose meaning on our observations of the physical world. In the words of Leonardo Da Vinci (1452–1519): "No human investigation can be called real science if it can-

Dr. Donald Pierce, affiliated with Western Oregon State University, contributed to this article.

not be demonstrated mathematically." Mathematics gives us a methodology for the collection and organization of data, as well as models and techniques that allow us to analyze and make predictions.

WHAT IS MATHEMATICS?

"Mathematics" means many things. It is a discipline, a science, an art, a language, a collection of techniques, and a way of thinking. Mathematics is a language of unparalleled precision; no other language allows us to communicate complex ideas with such specificity. Mathematics is a science of patterns, and, as such, is particularly well-suited for describing, defining, expressing, and answering questions about the natural world. According to astronomer Johannes Kepler, "The chief aim of all investigations of the external world should be to discover the rational order and harmony which has been imposed on it by God and which He revealed to us in the language of mathematics."

Mathematics is a science, but not an empirical science. In an empirical science nothing is ever proven. Observations yield evidence that may support or refute a theory, but no matter how well supported by data, no scientific theory is ever proven in the mathematical sense. In mathematics we start with clearly identified assumptions and proceed carefully, logically, in a reproducible way to a result. The result is absolutely certain, predicated only on the initial assumptions made and a universe where the rules of logic used in the process are valid. In the words of electrical engineer Charles Steinmetsz, "Mathematics is the most exact science, and its conclusions are capable of absolute proof. But this is so only because mathematics does not attempt to draw absolute conclusions. All mathematical truths are relative, conditional." Thus, though mathematics is useful in the physical world, it is independent of physical reality.

This independence from physical reality prompted the English mathematician and philosopher Alfred North Whitehead to describe mathematics as "thought moving in the sphere of complete abstraction independent of any particular instance of what it is talking about." The English poet William Wordsworth described mathematics as "an independent world . . . created out of pure intelligence." Yet mathematics is not without applications, and mathematical models often suggest interactions in the real world. Neptune, for example, was discovered by mathematics. The existence and exact location of Neptune was demonstrated with pencil and paper; all that was left to observers was to turn their telescopes to the proper location. To physicist Freeman Dyson, "mathematics is not just a tool by means of which phenomena can be calculated, it is the main source of concepts and principles by means of which new theories can be created."

HISTORY AND BACKGROUND

Man first began to use tools about 35,000 years ago. These early humans were primarily nomadic hunters, dependent on migrating herds of animals for their survival. By 8000 B.C., primitive people had begun to develop more reliable sources of food through primitive forms of agriculture and animal husbandry.

Compelling archaeological evidence obtained from the walls of tombs, mummy wrappings, cave paintings, and carvings indicates the cultivation of figs, olives, pomegranates, and dates was well-established in the Near East by 6500 B.C. As societies grew so did their need to use numbers.

Mathematics in the ancient world was an applied science: volumes of granaries and buildings and the areas of fields had to be determined; accounts had to be reconciled; and taxes had to be collected. Problems involving division of a field and the size of bricks needed for construction led to algebraic and geometrical problems. The Egyptians developed an excellent working knowledge of geometry, as evidenced by such major civic constructions as the Sphinx and the pyramids. However, until the time of the Greeks, mathematics consisted of a collection of rule-of-thumb procedures arrived at through experimentation, observation, analogy, guessing and occasional flashes of intuition. The Greeks took these applied procedures, examined their validity and generality, and developed a theoretical basis that gave birth to the discipline of theoretical mathematics. The field of mathematics has continued to grow and diversify, developing hand in hand with the sciences. Seven branches of learning were studied in the Middle Ages: arithmetic, geometry, logic, grammar, rhetoric, astronomy, and music—more than half the curriculum involved mathematics.

MATHEMATICS TODAY

Mathematics plays an even larger role in our modern technological society. The ability to understand quantitative issues that involve mathematics, science, and technology is a critical skill for all citizens today—on and off the job. Environmental and fiscal policy issues facing today's electorate will profoundly affect our future quality of life. The world's population will likely double in the next 40 years, yet we are already expending energy at rates far beyond sustainable levels. Appropriate policies in response to such critical issues as an exponentially growing population, the allocation of dwindling natural resources, emissions of greenhouse gases, ozone depletion, and the "disposal" of nuclear waste must be established. The level of mathematical literacy needed to participate in the world, its jobs, its economic and social orders, and its democratic institutions has risen dramatically in the last few decades. Today mathematics is studied for its applicability and utility, for its beauty, and for the problem-solving skills its study develops.

WHAT COURSES DO YOU NEED TO TAKE?

Mathematics is a broad field, and the courses that are required for a degree vary from school to school; however, there are some core courses everyone majoring in mathematics should take. As soon as you are qualified, you should begin with the calculus sequence, which should take you about a year and a half. Generally, this sequence is all the mathematics that is recommended during your first year. In your later years you will probably have to take additional sequences in real analysis and abstract algebra, and select from many electives. These include:

Analytic Geometry and Calculus	Assembly Language
Applied Graph Theory	Computer Organization

Differential Equations
Euclidean and Non-Euclidean Geometry
Number Theory
Numerical Analysis

Probability and Statistics
Problem-Solving
Topology

WHAT CAN YOU DO WITH A DEGREE IN MATHEMATICS?

A strong mathematics background is essential for success in any of the science disciplines—natural and social. Students who major in mathematics often pursue advanced degrees in other disciplines: biology, chemistry, physics, statistics, business, and economics, to name just a few. Although these disciplines don't require an undergraduate degree in mathematics, the experts say that a mathematics background (either major or minor) will serve you well in these and many other disciplines. Although there are relatively few jobs that require advanced mathematics of the type studied by a math major, almost all employers realize mathematics majors are skilled problem-solvers and hard workers.

If you don't plan to go on to graduate school for a master's or doctorate, consider combining your study of mathematics with another discipline. If you like working with computers, there is no more employable degree than a major/minor combination of mathematics and computer science.

WHAT DO EXPERTS SAY ABOUT MATHEMATICS?

Dr. Donald Pierce, affiliated with Western Oregon State University, offers this advice for prospective students:

What can a person expect during the course of study? Many students find calculus difficult. Not only do you have to understand calculations and symbol manipulation, you also have to think conceptually more often than in prior course work. It is important that you get a firm grasp of the concepts encountered in calculus, as they will continue to surface again and again in later courses. Calculus is rich in applications and it is easy to understand how to use the information being learned, but as you begin to take upper division coursework, concepts will become increasingly abstract. You will need to develop a whole new way of problem-solving to do well in abstract mathematics. Learning to write mathematical proofs is very challenging for most students and it takes time to learn. In each field of mathematics there are certain base assumptions upon which the field is built. A mathematical proof means giving a clear argument that shows how the assertion you are attempting to prove follows from these assumptions or other previously proven consequences of these assumptions.

What are the characteristics of a successful student? Expect to work hard if you study mathematics. Don't settle for "just getting through" a course or topic, as the techniques you miss will likely be needed in other courses. If you want to succeed, you will need to live and breathe mathematics. That means going to bed at night pondering mathematical questions and jumping up to scribble an idea down whenever it occurs to you. Although the mathematics you have studied so far has probably seemed somewhat static, as you learn more advanced mathematics, you will come to view your understanding as dynamic. It becomes a voyage of discovery. Mathematics is not invented or created so much as discovered. One comes to see beauty in the field and develops an intuition for the kinds of structures that exist in abstract mathematics. You have to have good computational skills to get to this point, but for those that do, it is a rewarding field of study.

What do you see for the future of the discipline? The future of mathematics is certain; it is a prerequisite to all the sciences, and science drives the high-tech world in which we live. Mathematics is developed and precedes applications, sometimes by many years.

What makes this field exciting to you, personally, and why do you love what you do? Rules and procedures are not all there is to mathematics. Like any other art, math has its own sense of aesthetics. Mathematical proofs require ingenuity and creativity; they are lasting works of art. When one reads a classic mathematical proof for the first time, such as Cantor's argument that the rational numbers are countable, you will be struck by the simplicity, ingenuity, and beauty of the mind that crafted the proof.

BEFORE YOU DECIDE . . .

Before you invest the next four years pursuing this field of study, invest a few hours in a thorough investigation of what a degree in mathematics can do for you. Use the following suggestions and the worksheet at the end of this chapter to make a plan for conducting some field research. Once your plan is complete and approved by your instructor, proceed to Part 5, Field Research, where you'll find further instructions for making the most of these activities.

TALK ABOUT IT

Conduct interviews with the following three people (using the information included in the Field Research section in Part 5 of this book to guide your discussions):

- A senior completing a degree in mathematics
- A mathematics professor at your school
- A professional working in a mathematics-related career

READ ABOUT IT

Following is a book listing that provides an overview of possible career options for someone with a degree in mathematics.

- Burnett, Rebecca. *Careers for Number Crunchers.* Lincolnwood, IL: VGM Career Horizons, 1992.
- Huffman, Harry. *Math for Business Careers.* New York: Macmillan/McGraw Hill, 1995.
- Kantranowitz, Mark and Joann P. Degennaro. *The Prentice Hall Guide to Scholarships and Fellowships for Mathematics and Science: A Resource for Students Pursuing Careers in Mathematical Science.* New York: Prentice Hall, 1993.

- Parker, Marla. *She Does Math!: Real Life Problems from Women on the Job.* Washington, D.C.: Mathematical Association of America, 1995.
- Richardson, Peter. *Great Careers for People Interested in Math and Computers.* Detroit: UXL, 1997.
- *Seeking Employment in the Mathematical Sciences.* Providence, RI: Mathematical Sciences Employment Register, 1994.
- Sterrett, Andrew. *101 Careers in Mathematics.* Washington, D.C.: Mathematical Association of America, 1996.

EXPERIENCE IT

Seek out an opportunity to see what a degree in mathematics can do for you in the workplace. Arrange a tour, job-shadowing experience, or even a full-fledged internship at a place such as:

- An accounting firm
- A market research company
- A computer hardware manufacturing firm
- A software development company
- The purchasing department of a large corporation
- The urban planning office of a major city or county

Once you have scheduled a first appointment, use the information included in the Field Research section of this book to make the most of this experience.

EXPLORE THE OPTIONS

- Accountant
- Actuary
- Architect
- Artificial Intelligence Specialist
- College Professor
- Computer Analyst
- Computer Engineer
- Demographer
- Financial Analyst
- Geographer
- Market Analyst
- Marketing Researcher
- Mathematician
- Operations Manager
- Physicist
- Purchasing Agent
- Researcher
- Statistician
- Stockbroker
- Surveyor
- Teacher (K–12)
- Traffic Manager
- Underwriter
- Urban Planner

REFERENCE

Pierce, Donald, Ed Wright, and Leon Roland. *Mathematics for Life: A Foundation Course for Quantitative Literacy.* Upper Saddle River, NJ: Prentice Hall, 1997.

Now that you've learned a little about what a major in mathematics is like, think about what it means for you. Could this be a good choice for you? Can you say with reasonable certainty that it's not a good fit at all? Use the following planning worksheet to explain your response.

NO WAY!

Here are three reasons why I don't think this major would be a good choice for me.

_____

_____

_____

Stop! If you are sure this is not a major you want to pursue, don't waste another minute! Move on and explore another major.

A DEFINITE MAYBE

Here are three reasons why I think this major might be a good choice for me.

_____

_____

_____

Following are my plans to find out all I can about this major.

FIELD RESEARCH PROJECT 1: TALK ABOUT IT

I will use materials included in the Field Research section of this book (Part 5) to conduct interviews with the following people:

_____ Senior completing a major in mathematics

_____ Mathematics professor

_____ Mathematics professional

FIELD RESEARCH PROJECT 2: READ ABOUT IT

I will use the materials included in Part 5 of this book to review the following book(s) about potential career tracks:

_____

_____

FIELD RESEARCH PROJECT 3: EXPERIENCE IT

I have arranged a tour or job-shadowing experience at the following location and will use the materials included in Part 5 of this book to record my observations:

_____ Location

_____ Contact Person

_____ Date and Time of Appointment

FIELD RESEARCH PROJECT 4: EXPLORE THE OPTIONS

I want to find out all I can about the following career(s) and will use the materials included in Part 5 of this book to guide my investigation at the library and on the Internet:

_____ Career Choice #1

_____ Career Choice #2

- -

_____

Student's Name and Date

_____ Field Research Plan Approved

_____ Field Research Plan Not Approved

Because:

_____

_____

_____

Instructor's Signature and Date

- -

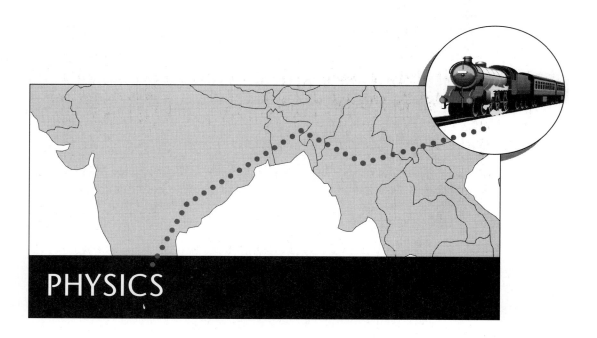

PHYSICS

Is This Major for You?

- Are you a logical thinker and a good problem-solver?
- Is your approach to completing work assignments well-organized and focused?
- Are you exceptionally good at math and totally interested in science?
- Can you stay motivated in a particular task to see it to completion even if it requires a good deal of time and painstaking work?
- Are you intrigued with the idea of being part of solving the mysteries of the universe?
- Are you interested in devoting your career to discovering new frontiers in areas such as nuclear energy, communications, the ocean, and space?
- Are you willing to consider alternative career paths to further the progression of your career (as many physicists report is a necessary element of their professional growth)?

If you answered yes to several of these questions, keep reading to find out if a major in physics is a good choice for you.

WHAT IS PHYSICS?

Physics is *the* basic science. Its goal is simple: to understand the rules of nature that govern the universe. Physicists hope that there are relatively few of these rules, applicable in general, and capable of explaining the widely diverse phenomena we observe, from everyday life, to stars, to DNA, indeed, to the universe itself.

Dr. Anthony Buffa, Physics Professor at California Polytechnic State University, contributed to this article.

Physics roughly separates into an experimental side and a theoretical side, although constant interaction between the two makes for a fuzzy dividing line. In some sense, physics is the ultimate exercise in philosophy asking fundamental questions, such as: What is the universe? How did it get here? What rules govern its operation? Where is it headed? Nowadays, of course, it is also separated along the lines of the practical versus the basic. Practical or applied physics, such as the study of the solid state that led to the discovery of the transistor and eventually to the microchip/computer revolution, leads to new technologies and inventions. Research in basic physics, for example, the study of elementary particle interactions, may also lead to new spin-off products for society, but its ultimate goal is more esoteric.

HISTORY AND BACKGROUND

For all of recorded history, man has been attempting to decipher the rules under which nature operates. The ancient Greeks had their laws of mechanics (which were, in fact, quite wrong!). Many scientists experimented with light, motion, sound, and heat. Some were in search of new and clever inventions, some were interested in using their ideas for global explorations, while still others were trying to understand the basic nature of things. Ancient astrologers evolved into modern-day astronomers and now astrophysicists.

At the end of the 19th century, it was mistakenly thought that the laws of physics had been found. In fact, nothing could have been further from the truth. The first half of the 20th century has often been called the "Golden Age of Physics." In this era we saw the birth of many revolutionary ideas that now shape our world: quantum mechanics, relativity, atomic physics, nuclear physics, cosmology, solid state physics, and more. Who could have foreseen these areas leading to laser surgery, high speed computers, the race to the moon, planetary exploration, and many other areas of endeavor we take for granted?

PHYSICS TODAY

In our modern world, physics takes on many different appearances. Yet all these aspects have the same fundamental glue. Physicists continue to delve into the ways things work. In today's world, you can find physicists at work in industry doing research on new technologies based on atomic, nuclear, and solid state physics. These technologies will shape our future world in ways we can only imagine. Other physicists are hard at work in the areas of basic research, for example, superconductivity, elementary particles, cosmology, quantum gravity, etc. Others are involved in teaching. They teach physics to nonscience and science/engineering majors, in classrooms ranging from elementary school to major research universities. You will also find physicists hard at work in biophysics and medical areas, making major strides in areas of health concerns. Many have gone into other fields such as management of large technical corporations, law practices, and medical practices. Physics today extends well beyond its past. Despite its diversity, physics continues its focus on learning about how things work.

WHAT COURSES DO YOU NEED TO TAKE?

Undergraduates usually take many courses in physics and mathematics, ranging from the introductory to advanced undergraduate. In physics, this includes such topics as classical and modern physics, electronics, optics, mechanics, quantum mechanics, electricity and magnetism, nuclear physics, elementary particle physics, astrophysics, solid state physics, and laser physics. In the area of mathematics, the courses start with calculus and move on to differential equations, matrices, linear algebra, complex variables, Fourier analysis, and computer programming techniques. Usually electives include a number of additional technical courses in such areas as chemistry and related engineering disciplines. Graduate courses usually are completed in the first two years. They are focused on physics and mathematics at the graduate level, covering similar topics but in much greater depth and sophistication than at the undergraduate level.

WHAT CAN YOU DO WITH A DEGREE IN PHYSICS?

At the bachelor's level, students are typically employed as engineers, teachers (with the addition of an appropriate teaching credential), or technicians. This degree can also serve as a stepping stone to graduate school in not only physics, but also engineering, other sciences, such as chemistry, and an M.B.A., M.D., or law school.

At the master's level, students are usually interested in industrial research, or teaching at a junior college or at the K–12 level. Many students at the M.S. level continue on for their Ph.D., the entire graduate program taking between four and eight years, depending on the subfield of research. With a Ph.D., the student would have access to university teaching and research professorships, and also industrial/governmental laboratory research. Government laboratories that hire a lot of Ph.D.s in physics include: Los Alamos National Laboratory in New Mexico, Argonne National Laboratory outside Chicago, and Brookhaven National Laboratory on Long Island, New York.

WHAT DO EXPERTS SAY ABOUT PHYSICS?

Dr. Anthony Buffa, Physics Professor at California Polytechnic State University, offers this advice to prospective students:

What can a person expect during the course of study in physics? At the undergraduate level, a typical degree program will include introductory classical physics, introductory modern physics, electronics, quantum mechanics, advanced mechanics, thermodynamics, electricity and magnetism, along with elective topics courses. The topics courses usually include nuclear and particle physics, solid state physics, laser physics, optics, and such. In addition to this, a physics major also takes a wide range of mathematics. Beginning with calculus, they then proceed through ordinary and partial differential equations, and also include courses in vector algebra and calculus, matrix methods, Fourier analysis, linear algebra, complex variables, and so on. If the student is in an applied physics option, other courses of a more applied nature are usually allowed as substitutes. This includes courses such as advanced electronics, electro-optics, robotics, computer programming and interfacing, and other courses taught in engineering departments.

At the graduate level, the programs are usually focused on preparing the student for a degree in research at the university, industrial, or government laboratory setting. Usually there are about two years of graduate courses required, among them, graduate level quantum mechanics and field theory, solid state physics, elementary particle physics, thermodynamics, and so on, along with more advanced mathematics and computer courses. To attain the degree of Doctor of Philosophy in Physics (Ph.D.), a research thesis acceptable in a refereed journal is required.

What are the characteristics of a successful student in physics? There are many different types of successful physics students. Typically they are well organized, can think logically, have a knack for solving problems (both on paper and in the lab), and can translate from a situation (words or laboratory) into the language of physics—mathematics.

What are the future opportunities in the field of physics? In the research area of physics, much depends on government funding of basic research, especially those areas not viewed as directly applied in nature, such as cosmology, planetary exploration, studies of the earth's interior, and elementary particle theory and experiment. In the applied areas, industry provides the research support in hopes of producing more and better products.

At the university level, it is predicted that aging professors will need to be replaced in great numbers in the next few decades, thus opening up opportunities for recent young Ph.Ds. For B.S. and M.S. degrees, there are expected to be many openings for teachers at the K–12 and junior college level. Many times B.S. and M.S. people also are hired by industry in engineering and research capacities, especially if their experience is in the experimental or computer areas.

What are some of the challenges facing physics? Adequate funding at all levels, in research, engineering, and teaching, is required for the field to continue to advance. It is not clear that university faculty positions will be available as university budgets shrink in real dollars. However, with the advent of the high technology society we now live in, there seems to be more and more industrial/government research laboratory opportunities, particularly in applied physics, which has an engineering bent.

What makes you passionate about physics? Why did you choose it? There is no doubt that physics is *the* fundamental science, upon which all other sciences and technologies are based. Its fundamental purpose is to find out how the universe works and the few laws that govern all the widely different physical phenomena we observe, from black holes to automobiles, dust particles, atoms, molecules, nuclei, and elementary particles. To me, it was intriguing because, at least in theory, one needs to know only a few fundamental "rules of the game" in order to understand the entire universe in which we live. What could be more interesting!

Is there any section or passage from your book that you think would be helpful to a prospective student? Our book is designed for nonmajors, mostly those in the areas of technology, biology, premedicine, and preveterinary medicine. Thus it does not speak specifically to those wanting to be physics majors. It is intended for those who are not physics majors. So I do not think there is an appropriate passage. You might consult an engineering/science text like Thornton, et al. (Prentice-Hall).

BEFORE YOU DECIDE . . .

Before you invest the next four years pursuing this field of study, invest a few hours in a thorough investigation of what a degree in physics can do for you. Use the following suggestions and the worksheet at the end of this chapter to make a plan for conducting some field research. Once your plan is complete and approved by your instructor, proceed to part 5, Field Research, where you'll find further instructions for making the most of these activities.

TALK ABOUT IT

Conduct interviews with the following three people (using the information included in the Field Research section in Part 5 of this book to guide your discussions):

- A senior completing a degree in physics
- A physics professor at your school
- A professional working in a physics-related career

READ ABOUT IT

Following is a book listing that provides an overview of possible career options for someone with a degree in physics.

- Easton, Thomas. *Careers in Science.* Indianapolis, IN: JIST, 1990.
- Ferbelman. Peter J. *A Ph.D. Is Not Enough: A Guide to Survival in Science.* Menlo Park, CA: Addison-Wesley, 1994.
- *Graduate Programs in Physics, Astronomy and Related Fields.* Woodbury, NY: American Institute of Physics, 1997.
- Morgan, Bradley J. and Joseph M. Palmisano, eds. *Physical Sciences Career Directory.* Detroit: Visible Ink Press, 1994.
- *Physics Careers: Employment and Education.* Woodbury, NY: American Institute of Physics, 1998.
- Robbins-Roth, Cynthia. *Alternative Careers in Science: Leaving the Ivory Tower.* San Diego: Academic Press, 1998.
- Rosen, Stephen and Celia Paul. *Career Renewal: Tools for Scientists and Technical Professionals.* San Diego: Academic Press, 1997.
- Sindermann, Carl J. and Thomas K. Sawyer. *The Scientist as Consultant: Building New Career Opportunities.* New York: Plenum Press, 1997.

EXPERIENCE IT

Seek out an opportunity to see what a degree in physics can do for you in the workplace. Arrange a tour, a job-shadowing experience, or even a full-fledged internship at a place such as:

- A planetarium
- An aerospace research facility
- A nuclear power plant
- A medical research laboratory
- An alternative energy research laboratory
- A communications research and development facility

Once you have scheduled a first appointment, use the information included in the Field Research section of this book to make the most of this experience.

EXPLORE THE OPTIONS

Using the materials included in the Field Research section at the end of this book, conduct a thorough investigation of at least two career options for college graduates with a physics degree. You'll need a good selection of career books and resources and access to the Internet to complete this task. Here are some ways to put a degree in physics to work. Use this list for ideas but feel free to focus your exploration on another idea that interests you.

- Acoustics Engineer
- Aerospace Engineer
- Astronomer
- Biophysicist
- College Professor
- Computer Engineer
- Computer Programmer
- Energy Engineer
- Geologist
- Geophysicist
- Lab Supervisor
- Mathematician
- Medical Physicist
- Metallurgical and Materials Engineer
- Nuclear Engineer
- Physicist
- Planetary Scientist
- Researcher
- Scientific Journalist
- Teacher (K–12)
- Technical Writer

REFERENCE

Wilson, Jerry and Anthony Buffa. *College Physics.* Upper Saddle River, NJ: Prentice Hall, 1996.

Now that you've learned a little about what a major in physics is like, think about what it means for you. Could this be a good choice? Can you say with reasonable certainty that it's not a good fit at all? Use the following planning worksheet to explain your response.

NO WAY!

Here are three reasons why I don't think this major would be a good choice for me.

_____

_____

_____

Stop! If you are sure this is not a major you want to pursue, don't waste another minute! Move on and explore another major.

A DEFINITE MAYBE

Here are three reasons why I think this major might be a good choice for me.

_____

_____

_____

Following are my plans to find out all I can about this major.

FIELD RESEARCH PROJECT 1: TALK ABOUT IT

I will use materials included in the Field Research section of this book (Part 5) to conduct interviews with the following people:

_____ Senior completing a major in physics

_____ Physics professor

_____ Physics professional

FIELD RESEARCH PROJECT 2: READ ABOUT IT

I will use the materials included in Part 5 of this book to review the following book(s) about potential career tracks:

_____

_____

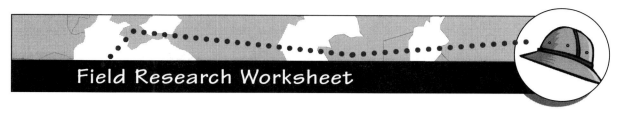

FIELD RESEARCH PROJECT 3: EXPERIENCE IT

I have arranged a tour or job-shadowing experience at the following location and will use the materials included in Part 5 of this book to record my observations:

_____ Location

_____ Contact Person

_____ Date and Time of Appointment

FIELD RESEARCH PROJECT 4: EXPLORE THE OPTIONS

I want to find out all I can about the following career(s) and will use the materials included in the Field Research section of this book to guide my investigation at the library and on the Internet:

_____ Career Choice #1

_____ Career Choice #2

_____

Student's Name and Date

_____ Field Research Plan Approved
_____ Field Research Plan Not Approved

Because:

_____

_____

_____

Instructor's Signature and Date

2 Humanities and Social Sciences

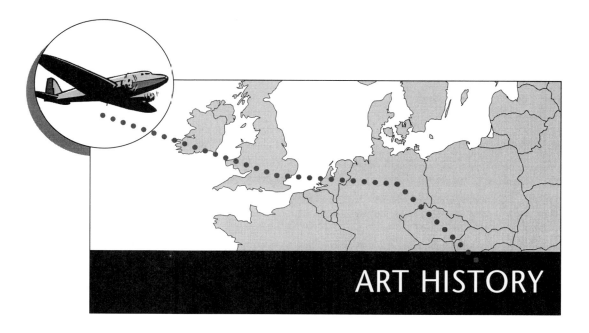

ART HISTORY

Is This Major for You?

- Do you have a passion for the arts?
- Can you think of creative ways to put your passion for art to work?
- Are you prepared to blend your interest in art with other marketable skills?
- Does the possibility of opening your mind to a new way of thinking and looking at life interest you?
- Are art museums, art galleries, concerts, and other "cultural" types of events among your favorite places to be?
- Do you have a genuine appreciation for the hard work and talent behind great works of art?
- Do you possess at least a tiny bit of natural artistic talent?
- Do you enjoy expressing yourself creatively?

If you answered yes to several of these questions, keep reading and find out if an art history major is a good choice for you.

INTRODUCTION

What is art? Few questions provoke as much debate and provide so few satisfactory answers. First of all art is a *word* that acknowledges both the *idea* and the *fact* of art. Without the word, one might ask whether art exists in the first place. The term is not found in every society. Yet, art is made everywhere. Art, therefore, is also an object, but not just any kind of object. Art is an aesthetic object, meant to be looked at and appreciated for its intrinsic value. Its special qualities set it apart so that it is often placed away from everyday life, in museums, caves,

Dr. Henry Sayre, Art History Professor at Oregon State University, contributed to this article.

or churches. Art captures the imagination, creativity, originality, and self-expression of the people and cultures that produce it. The study of art history helps students to develop a sense of self-expression and who they are by helping them analyze and appreciate art across the ages.

WHAT IS ART HISTORY?

Art history is, first, the study of artistic style through which meaning is expressed, resulting in an art object. Second, art history is the social, political, and historical context in which the art was created. Works of art are studied on their own terms as objects of beauty (aesthetic objects) and as cultural artifacts, as history, reflecting and embodying the issues of the day.

Art history can reveal to us not only the terms in which cultures define their highest achievements—their masterpieces—but how those definitions change over time, and how works of art continue to express the "human condition." The study of art history reveals ourselves to ourselves—the words that Paul Gauguin employed to title his great painting, *Where Do We Come From? Where Are We? Where Are We Going?* In the broadest sense, art history is an exercise in self-knowledge.

HISTORY AND BACKGROUND

The history of art is a comparatively young discipline. The term "history of art" first appears in the writing of German Johan Winckleman in his *History of Ancient Art,* which appeared in 1764 and which resulted from his supervision of excavations in Rome, Herculaneum, and Pompeii. In the first decades of the 19th century, professorships in the study of art were established in Germany, and the first person to hold the title Professor of the History of Art was Franz Kugler, who taught at the Academy of Art in Berlin.

In the middle of the 19th century, Ivy League schools inaugurated art history programs, and lectureships in art history were established in other universities as well. In its earliest days, art history sought to distinguish itself from archeology and the study of the classics by emphasizing the formal aspects of studying the art object. In form, and in the history of form, it was believed universal truths could be discovered. In 1874, Harvard Professor of Fine Arts Charles Eliot Norton said "There cannot be . . . good paintings or sculpture, or architecture, unless [people] have something to express which is the result of long training of soul and sense in the ways of high living and true thought."

Art history's function as trainer of soul and sense, as arbiter of good taste and true thought, was broadened in the 1930s when many of Germany's best art historians immigrated to America in order to escape Nazi persecution. German art history had long been an interdisciplinary field, informed by sociology, economics, philosophy and linguistics, history, and especially philosophy. These historians introduced a theoretical and social-historical approach to the formalist tradition in America. Art history has since been defined by both groups, who for many years were in opposition but recently have achieved a courteous coexistence.

ART HISTORY TODAY

In recent years, art history has been increasingly concerned with its isolation as a discipline—that is, with the particularly male, Western point of view that has traditionally informed it. Gender studies, and the expressions of ethnic, marginalized, and non-European traditions have become increasingly important areas of study. Art historians today study the marketplace, patronage systems, and the economics of distribution in order to understand, through art, the power exerted by "high" culture. New areas of artistic endeavor—television, film, the computer, digital technologies, and the Internet—are redefining and its audience. The understanding of visual culture and the history of visual literacy are today art history's true domain.

WHAT COURSES DO YOU NEED TO TAKE?

Art history today is taught in one of two ways. The institution you choose may have an art history department, or art history may be part of the fine arts department. Regardless of the path you take, the following requirements and electives are generally offered:

Baroque Art	Indian Art
Chinese Art	Modern Art
Gender Issues in Art	19th Century American Art
Greek/Classical Art	Renaissance Art
History of Western Art	

Various courses that address other ethnic and non-European traditions are also offered.

WHAT CAN YOU DO WITH A DEGREE IN ART HISTORY?

Art history has long carried the stigma of being an impractical discipline, a refined course of study, training its students, in Charles Eliot Norton's words, "in the ways of high living and true thought." But, as art history increasingly confronts the cultural (and class) biases behind such assumptions, it has become an increasingly engaged, rich field of cultural study.

Job opportunities in the field, however, remain relatively slim. As museums feel the pressure of decreased public funding, fewer curatorial positions are available. There are some opportunities with galleries in the private sector, but the wisest approach is to be versatile. Students seeking jobs in the private sector should think about minoring in business, with a marketing and accounting emphasis. Conversely, an art minor with a business major can lead to employment opportunities in institutional development and marketing for museums, as well as the private sector.

Many of the employment opportunities today are for individuals with degrees in graphic arts. Art history provides graphic designers and fine artists with the self-knowledge that allows them to create art with a self-critical sense.

A major in art history trains you to do virtually any job that requires rigorous and creative thinking. Many employers recognize this and routinely hire undergraduate art majors to work in a wide variety of fields. They realize that they can train you in the particulars of their business, but that they cannot train you to think well; art history trains people to think.

WHAT DO EXPERTS SAY ABOUT ART HISTORY?

Dr. Henry Sayre, Professor of Art History at Oregon State University, offers this advice to prospective students:

What can a person expect during this course of study? Many students are shocked to discover that pursuing art history requires memorization work. Students must know and identify great works of traditional art. They must learn how to look at a work of art, to understand how and why it was created. They learn what philosophical and cultural assumptions were behind the choices.

What are the characteristics of a successful student? The main characteristic of the successful student is a good visual memory.

What do you see for the future of the discipline? The future of the discipline rests with the changes in our culture. The culture as a whole is becoming increasingly visually oriented. Analysis of visual rhetoric is becoming increasingly important to an understanding of what is happening in the world. Visual culture is important—that's the direction the discipline will go.

What makes the field exciting to you, personally, and why do you love what you do? I came to the discipline because it seemed to be the place where a lot was being said and discovered about culture, whether 17th century or the present. As a writer, I felt there were lots of opportunities for people to articulate about art history, which would provide a broad perspective about the culture. There is a weakness in jargon-laden writing about art history that has traditionally been produced. I see great opportunities to help change that.

BEFORE YOU DECIDE . . .

Before you invest the next four years pursuing this field of study, invest a few hours in a thorough investigation of what a degree in art history can do for you. Use the following suggestions and the worksheet at the end of this chapter to make a plan for conducting some field research. Once your plan is complete and approved by your instructor, proceed to Part 5, Field Research, where you'll find further instructions for making the most of these activities.

TALK ABOUT IT

Conduct interviews with the following three people (using the information included in the Field Research section to guide your discussions):

- A senior completing a major in art history

- An art history professor at your school
- A professional working in an art-related career

READ ABOUT IT

Following is a book list that provides an overview of possible career options for someone with a degree in art history.

- Bates, G.W. *Museum Jobs from A to Z.* Switzerland: Batax Museum Publishers, 1994.
- *Career Choices for Students of Art.* New York: Walker and Co., 1990.
- Eberts, Marjorie and Margaret Gisler. *Careers for Bookworms and Other Literary Types.* Lincolnwood, IL: VGM Career Horizons, 1996.
- Eberts, Marjorie and Margaret Gisler. *Careers for Culture Lovers and Other Artsy Types.* Lincolnwood, IL: VGM Career Horizons, 1997.
- Grant, Daniel. *On Becoming an Artist.* New York: Allworth Press, 1993.
- Haubenstock, Susan H. and David Joselit. *Career Opportunities in Art.* New York: Facts on File, 1994.
- Holden, Don. *Art Career Guide.* New York: Watson-Guptill Publications, 1983.
- Langley, Stephen and James Abruzzo. *Jobs in Arts and Media Management: What They Are and How to Get One.* New York: American Council for the Arts, 1986.
- Schmidt, Peggy. *Career Choices for the 90's: Art.* New York: Walker, 1990.

EXPERIENCE IT

Seek out an opportunity to see what a degree in art history can do for you in the workplace. Arrange a tour, a job-shadowing experience, or even a full-fledged internship at a place such as:

- The art department of an advertising agency
- A fine arts gallery
- An art museum
- A publisher of books, magazines, or newspapers
- A self-employed graphic designer or book illustrator

Once you have scheduled a first appointment, use the information included in the Field Research section to make the most of this experience.

EXPLORE THE OPTIONS

Using the materials included in the Field Research section, conduct a thorough investigation of at least two career options for college graduates with an art history degree. You'll need a good selection of career books and resources and access to the Internet to complete this task. Here are some ways to put a degree in art history to work. Use this list for ideas but feel free to focus your exploration on another idea that interests you.

- Advertising Account Executive
- Appraiser
- Architect
- Art Critic
- Art Director
- Artist
- Arts Administrator
- Auctioneer
- Book Illustrator
- Cartoonist
- Conservator
- Costume Designer
- Editor
- Exhibit Designer
- Fashion Designer
- Film Producer
- Graphic Designer
- Industrial Designer
- Information Specialist
- Interior Designer
- Journalist
- Librarian
- Multi-Media Project Designer
- Museum Curator
- Museum Educator
- Nonprofit Agency Director

REFERENCES

Janson, Anthony F. *History of Art.* Upper Saddle River, NJ: Prentice Hall, 1997.
Sayre, Henry. *A World of Art.* Upper Saddle River, NJ: Prentice Hall, 1996.

Now that you've learned a little about what a major in art history is like, think about what it means for you. Could this be a good choice for you? Can you say with reasonable certainty that it's not a good fit at all? Use the following planning worksheet to explain your response.

NO WAY!

Here are three reasons why I don't think this major would be a good choice for me.

_____

_____

_____

Stop! If you are sure this is not a major you want to pursue, don't waste another minute! Move on and explore another major.

A DEFINITE MAYBE

Here are three reasons why I think this major might be a good choice for me.

_____

_____

_____

Following are my plans to find out all I can about this major.

FIELD RESEARCH PROJECT 1: TALK ABOUT IT

I will use the materials in the Field Research section of this book (Part 5) to conduct interviews with the following people:

_____ Senior completing a major in art history

_____ Art history professor

_____ Art history professional

FIELD RESEARCH PROJECT 2: READ ABOUT IT

I will use Part 5 of this book to review the following book(s) about potential career tracks:

_____

_____

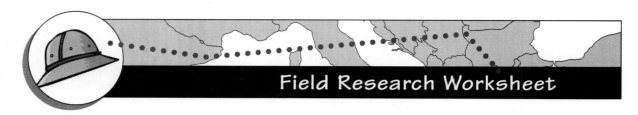

FIELD RESEARCH PROJECT 3: EXPERIENCE IT

I have arranged a tour or job-shadowing experience at the following location and will use Part 5 of this book to record my observations:

_____ Location

_____ Contact Person

_____ Date and Time of Appointment

FIELD RESEARCH PROJECT 4: EXPLORE THE OPTIONS

I want to find out all I can about the following career(s) and will use Part 5 of this book to guide my investigation at the library and on the Internet:

_____ Career Choice #1

_____ Career Choice #2

· ·

_____

Student's Name and Date

_____ Field Research Plan Approved

_____ Field Research Plan Not Approved

Because:

_____

_____

_____

Instructor's Signature and Date

· ·

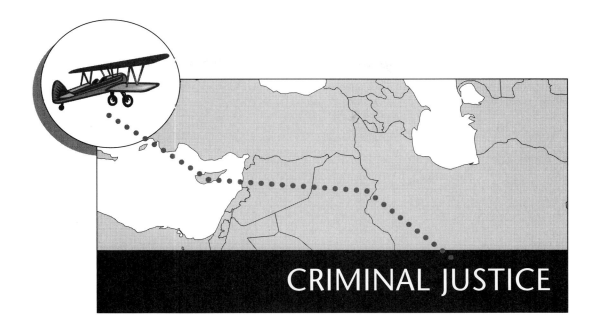

CRIMINAL JUSTICE

Is This Major for You?

- Are you a natural leader?
- Do you tend to take charge of situations—deciding where to go out to eat, making a game plan, etc.?
- Do you have a genuine interest in helping other people?
- Do you have a calm, diplomatic approach to dealing with tense situations?
- Are you able to see both sides of the story in a dispute?
- Does curling up with a good mystery sound like fun to you?
- Do you like trying to figure out "who dunnit" in mysteries and detective shows?
- Does the idea of serving and protecting others appeal to you even if it means laying your life on the line?
- Do you have a strong sense of right and wrong?
- Is justice an important value in your life?

If you answered yes to several of these questions, keep reading and find out if a criminal justice major is a good choice for you.

INTRODUCTION

Recently released crime rate data show heartening statistical reductions in some reporting categories, but crime remains a major problem in American society. Law-abiding citizen and lawbreaker alike devour television programs like *Cops*

Gordon Armstrong, Criminal Justice Professor at Georgia State University, contributed to this article.

and *America's Most Wanted*. Arrogant, youthful parolees often return to a hero's welcome in their neighborhoods. Because prisons remain grossly overcrowded, criminals laugh at the system, accepting jail sentences over probation, which leads to a quicker release. Though the criminal justice system in America seems a hopeless mess, its problems are nevertheless manageable. Fresh perspectives from people entering this field are the key to solving them.

WHAT IS CRIMINAL JUSTICE?

Criminal justice addresses crime in society. It deals with the systems of a society to contain crime. Crime rates rise and fall, and while it can never really be eliminated as long as there are human beings in society, it can be contained at a tolerable level. If crime touches you personally, you may think that it is intolerable no matter what statistics say, but given the population as a whole, keeping crime to a manageable level is what criminal justice is all about. Criminal justice is different than criminology: criminology seeks to answer why human beings do what they do. Criminology deals with the causations of crime; criminal justice deals with the existence of it.

HISTORY AND BACKGROUND

Human beings possess an element of inherent selfishness, and as long as there have been human beings living in association, there has been crime. The ways in which groups deal with crime evolve with the society. Before organized communities with no formal social structure, pockets of people were self-sustaining; they fended for themselves in the field of justice. Punishment for crimes was usually dispatched on the spot, and no one worried about retaliation to the punishers.

When frontier settings were absorbed by civilization, better policing methods were needed to maintain order and fairness. Urban centers needed a governing infrastructure to bring peace to the community. The first formal policing agency was formed in England in 1829. The Metropolitan Police Force of London became the model after which many other organizations were formed, including the first police force in New York in 1844. The London model incorporated a number of unique features: (1) like the army, the force had a hierarchy of command to promote order; (2) members wore uniforms, including a hat, to be detected by citizens and one another, and to be intimidating; (3) individuals on the original force were over six feet tall so that they would be physically intimidating. The uniforms had a row of copper buttons down the front, hence the nickname "coppers" and "cops." Officers were assigned a certain patrol area in order to know the people on their "beat"—who was a criminal and who was not. One American modification to the British system was the decentralization of operations of the various precincts. Each was expected to uphold certain rules, but how that was accomplished was decided by each precinct. It became easy for police departments in large metropolitan areas to be influenced by local political activity, and many police forces based their activities on what politicians wanted. Political influence has largely disappeared from the ranks, and police are left with the daunting task of maintaining peace as we approach the year 2000.

CRIMINAL JUSTICE TODAY

The single most influential factor that makes crime rates appear to be so high today is communication. Today's media bring every gruesome detail of crimes into our lives within seconds of occurrence, sometimes even as they occur. If we compare crime rates across time, geography, and topography, today's rates are no different proportionately than those of one hundred years ago. If in a town of 100, one person is killed, one percent of the population is a murder victim. If one percent of the population of New York were killed, the number of victims would be nearly 80,000. In actuality, only a fraction of that number are indeed murdered. Statistics can be misleading if misinterpreted, and this misinterpretation can be dangerous if people are not aware of how the numbers are derived. This is not meant to discount the loss of life to killings but to take a responsible look at how the media choose to portray the crime picture in this country. Criminal justice today is composed of three areas: law enforcement, the courts, and corrections.

LAW ENFORCEMENT. Involves controlling societal behavior; polices citizens to comply with the law. When there is a crime, law enforcement personnel determine who did it, why they did it, how they did it, and turn the information over to the courts. Law enforcement organizations may be governmental, private security, or investigating firms.

COURTS. Sift through the information presented and seek to identify that a crime did indeed occur—you can't have a violation if there's no valid law to violate. If there is a violation, the case goes to trial before a jury and a verdict is achieved. If the verdict is "not guilty," the criminal event is over. If the verdict is "guilty," the next step is corrections.

CORRECTIONS. Carries out the level of state control of behavior over time, which includes overseeing probation, parole, jail, and prison sentences. The least level of correction is an admonishment by the judge; the highest level of control is execution. From community service programs to solitary confinement in a maximum security prison, corrections seeks to deliver criminals out of the system as economically as possible.

Today a raging debate exists between keeping public order and maintaining individual rights. Many citizens are angry because repeat offenders are set free to perpetrate again due to prison overcrowding. Why would anyone choose to major in a field that is viewed negatively by increasing numbers of Americans? Many people do not stop to think that, despite its imperfections, our criminal justice system works. The Constitution outlined a clear set of rules that extends to every citizen called due process: if you commit an offense, you will be arrested, you will be tried, and you will be punished. Upon completion of this process, you are set free. The system cannot keep you on the fact that you might offend again. The founding fathers deliberately skewed the system in favor of the criminal to keep innocent people from being arrested and punished. They felt it was far more injurious to punish the innocent than to let a guilty individual go. Be glad this is so. Once greater limits are applied to bad behavior, there is greater intrusion on individual rights. For example, consider airport travel. At one time, travelers could board planes with no hassles whatsoever. That is not the case anymore. And once the powers that be intrude upon individuals' rights, where does it stop? Adolph Hitler took the helm in Germany and selectively pruned away constitutional rights until some groups did not have any left.

There are no quick fixes to the problems that crime creates in this country. The problems cannot be changed by decree or consensus, but they can be addressed and contained. The field is challenging and needs individuals who believe in the system our founding fathers envisioned would provide "liberty and justice for all."

WHAT COURSES DO YOU NEED TO TAKE?

Courses are designed to provide the student with a background in the many areas of employment that are available in this dynamic field. Depending on the program you choose, the following are included as requirements and electives:

Advanced Correction	Internships
American Criminal Court System	Introduction to Criminal Justice
Comparative Industrial Security	Justice and Ethics
Criminal Investigation	Juvenile Justice
Criminal Justice Management and Operations	Legal Aspects of Crime
	Offender Counseling and Support
Criminal Procedure	Organized Crime
Evidence	Police Administration
Gangs, Drugs, and Crime	Probation and Parole

WHAT CAN YOU DO WITH A DEGREE IN CRIMINAL JUSTICE?

Many people avoid criminal justice as a major consideration because they "don't want to be a cop." Criminal justice offers many opportunities in both public and private sectors. In law enforcement, in addition to being a cop, you can consider jobs ranging from child protective services investigator, to fishing industry investigator for the U. S. Fish and Wildlife Service. In court work, there are bailiffs, court administrators, docket managers, legal stenographers or clerks, pre-sentencing investigators, and many support positions in approximately 17,000 general, limited, and appellate courts throughout the nation. In corrections, jails, prisons, probation and parole offices, and a myriad of community correctional and counseling facilities need individuals in every imaginable position from warden to drug rehab counselor to prisoner intake and classification specialist. Community corrections programs need talented administrators with an education or experience in criminal justice. For more investigation, visit http://www.stpt./usf.edu/~greek/cj.html.

WHAT DO EXPERTS SAY ABOUT CRIMINAL JUSTICE?

Gordon Armstrong, Criminal Justice Professor at Georgia Southern University, offers this advice to prospective students:

What can you expect from the course of study? In addition to courses in criminal justice, students should take an interdisciplinary approach and include courses in sociology and political science. Individuals in this field need to understand how the country and the society work. If students want to be leaders in this field, they should include business and computer courses so they can reach beyond being solely functionaries.

What are the characteristics of a successful student? A successful student places studies first and maintains a balance between social and academic life. They should approach studies with a desire to gain knowledge and not just gain a credential. Successful students are socially aware and socially concerned. They see criminal justice for what it is—a growth industry. They are not naive enough to believe they can solve the crime problem, but they know they can help contain it.

What do you see for the future of the discipline? The future will see a major transition toward the use of technology to pursue criminals. Information is what you need to solve a crime and technology provides that access. For example, the technology used in DNA profiling has been used to exonerate one out of four people arrested for crimes they did not commit. Another aspect in the future of this field is understanding social changes—as the social and racial demographics in this country change, crime will change too.

What makes the field exciting to you, personally, and why do you love what you do? I am committed to this field because it is a service field. There is more to life than working for money. This field makes a contribution to the national community—it is an opportunity to contribute in the sense of "I have served."

BEFORE YOU DECIDE . . .

Before you invest the next four years pursuing this field of study, invest a few hours in a thorough investigation of what a degree in criminal justice can do for you. Use the following suggestions and the worksheet at the end of this chapter to make a plan for conducting some field research. Once your plan is complete and approved by your instructor, proceed to Part 5 Field Research, where you'll find further instructions for making the most of these activities.

TALK ABOUT IT

Conduct interviews with the following three people (using the information included in the Field Research section to guide your discussions):

- A senior completing a major in criminal justice
- A criminal justice professor at your school
- A professional working in a criminal justice–related career

READ ABOUT IT

Following is a book listing that provides an overview of possible career options for someone with a degree in criminal justice.

- Henry, Stuart. *Inside Jobs: A Realistic Guide to Criminal Justice Careers for College Graduates*. Salem, WI: Sheffield Publishing Company, 1994.
- Hesalroad, Mary N. *Law Enforcement Career Starter*. New York: Learning Express, 1998.

- Hutton, Donald. *Guide to Law Enforcement Careers*. Hauppauge, NYk: Barron's Educational Series, 1991.
- Lee, Mary Price. *100 Best Careers in Crime Fighting, Law Enforcement, Criminal Justice, Private Security and Cyberspace Crime Detection*. New York: Macmillan, 1998.
- Smith, Russ. *Federal Jobs in Law Enforcement*. Manassas Park, VA: Impact Publications, 1996.
- Stinchcomb, James. *Opportunities in Law Enforcement and Criminal Justice Careers*. Lincolnwood, IL: VGM Career Horizons, 1996.

EXPERIENCE IT

Seek out an opportunity to see what a degree in criminal justice can do for you in the workplace. Arrange a tour, a job-shadowing experience, or even a full-fledged internship at a place such as:

- A juvenile detention center
- A courthouse
- A police department
- A coroner's office
- A federal agency such as the FBI
- A law firm

Once you have scheduled a first appointment, use the information in the Field Research section to make the most of this experience.

EXPLORE THE OPTIONS

Using the materials included in the Field Research section, conduct a thorough investigation of at least two career options for college graduates with a criminal justice degree. You'll need a good selection of career books and resources and access to the Internet to complete this task.

Here are some ways to put a degree in criminal justice to work. Use this list for ideas but feel free to focus your exploration on another idea that interests you.

- Attorney
- Bailiff
- Coroner
- Corrections Officer
- Court Administrator
- Court Reporter
- Detective
- Docket Manager
- Federal Agent (FBI, CIA, IRS, etc.)
- Forensics Investigator
- Insurance Investigator
- Investigative Reporter
- Judge
- Legal Clerk
- Paralegal
- Police Officer
- Private Investigator
- Warden

REFERENCE

Armstrong, Gordon. *Career Paths: A Guide to Employment Opportunities in Criminal Justice*. Upper Saddle River, NJ: Prentice Hall, 1997.

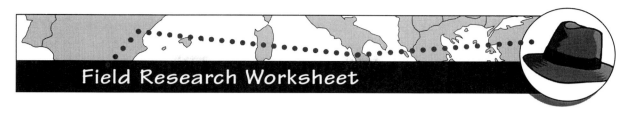

Now that you've learned a little about what a major in criminal justice is like, think about what it means for you. Could this be a good choice? Can you say with reasonable certainty that it's not a good fit at all? Use the following planning worksheet to explain your response.

NO WAY!

Here are three reasons why I don't think this major would be a good choice for me.

_____

_____

_____

Stop! If you are sure this is not a major you want to pursue, don't waste another minute! Move on and explore another major.

A DEFINITE MAYBE

Here are three reasons why I think this major might be a good choice for me.

_____

_____

_____

Following are my plans to find out all I can about this major.

FIELD RESEARCH PROJECT 1: TALK ABOUT IT

I will use the materials in the Field Research section of this book (Part 5) to conduct interviews with the following people:

_____ Senior completing a major in criminal justice

_____ Criminal justice professor

_____ Criminal justice professional

FIELD RESEARCH PROJECT 2: READ ABOUT IT

I will use Part 5 of this book to review the following book(s) about potential career tracks:

_____

_____

FIELD RESEARCH PROJECT 3: EXPERIENCE IT

I have arranged a tour or job-shadowing experience at the following location and will use Part 5 of this book to record my observations:

_____ Location

_____ Contact Person

_____ Date and Time of Appointment

FIELD RESEARCH PROJECT 4: EXPLORE THE OPTIONS

I want to find out all I can about the following career(s) and will use Part 5 of this book to guide my investigation at the library and on the Internet:

_____ Career Choice #1

_____ Career Choice #2

_____

Student's Name and Date

_____ Field Research Plan Approved

_____ Field Research Plan Not Approved

Because:

_____

_____

_____

Instructor's Signature and Date

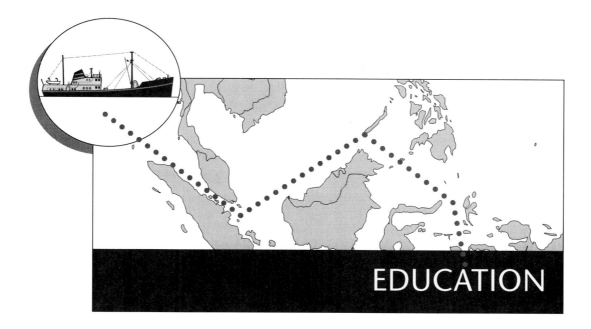

EDUCATION

Is This Major for You?

- Are you good at explaining things in a way that other people can understand?
- Do you have an insatiable urge to learn new things?
- Do you enjoy—really enjoy—working with people of a certain age whether it's children, adults, special needs populations, or teenagers?
- Are you a good student who values the educational process?
- Are you willing to learn how to speak effectively in front of other people?
- Can you fairly and objectively evaluate the work of others; are you able to set aside your own need to be liked in order to help them achieve their personal best?
- Are you well-organized and able to focus your attention?

If you answered yes to several of these questions, keep reading to find out if an education major is a good choice for you.

INTRODUCTION

Renowned anthropologist Margaret Mead said, "In this world, no one can complete an education." How true. Today, more than ever before, education is a lifelong endeavor. Graduation from college no longer means that you are launched into the world to pursue your career, never to return to the classroom. Today's ever-changing technological and economic conditions require individuals of all ages and circumstances to continually update and enhance their skills.

Dr. Richard Kellough, Education Professor at California State University at Sacramento, contributed to this article.

The challenge for educators today is to meet the demands of students from preschool through retirement and beyond.

WHAT IS EDUCATION?

Education is the process by which people acquire knowledge, skills, habits, values, and attitudes. It involves both teaching and learning, and is indeed a life-long process. All of us are continually learning. Hindu leader Krishnamurti states, "There is no end to education. It is not that you read a book, pass an examination, and finish with education. The whole of life, from the moment you are born to the moment you die is a process of learning." Those involved in the business of formal education, the teachers, are the people to whom most of us look to find the spark of excitement that accompanies education.

HISTORY AND BACKGROUND

Education is as old as the human race. From prehistoric times through today, young people have been educated by their communities through apprenticeships, initiations, or rituals. Formal education as we think of it now did not begin until civilizations developed written language. Ancient Greek and Roman cultures taught children in philosophy, mathematics, rhetoric, government, and history.

Early Western education was closely associated with religion. Hebrew, Christian, and Muslim cultures developed educational systems that stressed sacred teachings as well as academics. During the Middle Ages in Europe, formal education was reserved for boys destined for religious service. Though universities teaching law and medicine started in the 1400s, these catered to upper-class males. Universal education for all children of all classes did not appear until the 1800s. In the United States, early colonists set up elementary schools that taught reading, writing, and religion. Many colonies required parents to teach their children to read. In the 1700s, colonies started secondary schools that taught subjects like bookkeeping and navigation, in addition to liberal arts. By the time the Revolutionary War ended in 1783, the United States had several universities.

Patriotism for the new country prompted efforts to create a unified nation. For education, this meant creating standardized textbooks and developing state public school systems. Educators promoted a view of the idealized American—excluding minority groups' perspectives—in an effort to give citizens a sense of national unity. All levels and kinds of education, including kindergarten, vocational schools, and junior colleges, grew as the country grew, and teachers stressed discipline and conformity.

After World War II, the educational system began to change. Enrollment increased, the cost of education increased, and teachers' organizations became militant about improving salaries and benefits for members. The federal government increased financial aid to public education and granted funds to veterans for higher education. Big changes occurred in *what* should be taught and *how* it should be taught. The 1970s brought heated debate between the formal, traditional approach (collective knowledge and skills) and a progressive, nontraditional approach (self-knowledge and personal skills). Ethnic minorities and women took advantage of opportunities previously denied them. Bilingual programs were established to accommodate non-English–speaking Americans.

EDUCATION TODAY

Education continues its transformation as the year 2000 approaches. The "relevance" of the 1960s has become the "connected learning" of today—helping students understand that their learning is connected to real life. Historically, educators thought they knew what students needed to know and what they wanted them to know for the purposes of creating community. The meaning of community in America has changed and education has had to respond. Regardless of the popular philosophy of the moment, the constants that remain are that students need to know how to learn, how to read, how to communicate, and how to think productively. To accomplish this is the challenge of education. The kinds of schooling available today, for students and teachers, would have amazed educators a century ago. In addition to a variety of technical schools, colleges, and universities, there are now a number of different kinds of K–12 facilities available. These include:

MAGNET SCHOOL. Specializes in a particular academic area, such as the visual and performing arts, science, mathematics and technology, or international studies. Magnet schools occur at all levels: elementary, middle, and high school.

PARTNERSHIP SCHOOL. Has entered into partnership with business and industry to link school studies with the community, parents, and the workplace.

TECH PREP. High school that has a 4+2 coordinated curriculum articulated from grades 9–12 to the first two years of college, leading to an Associate of Applied Science degree.

FULL-SERVICE SCHOOL. Offers quality education and comprehensive social services all under one roof.

CHARTER SCHOOL. Operates as an autonomous educational entity under a charter of contract that has been negotiated between the organizers who create and operate it and a sponsor who oversees the provisions of the charter. Charter schools are one of the fastest growing movements in the country in response to widespread dissatisfaction with public schools.

Another rapid change is in the number of schools that have changed from the traditional school year (September through June) to a year-round operation, some with variations from the traditional length of class periods. Between 1985–1995, the number of schools that changed to a year-round program increased from 410 in 16 states to more than 2,200 in 37 states. Many institutions are experiencing school restructuring, which involves changes in existing fundamental assumptions, practices, and relationships within the organization and between the organization and the outside community. Restructuring is meant to improve learning outcomes, and educators agree that the design and functions of schools should reflect the needs of today's students rather than those of the 19th century. The purpose of school reform efforts and of school restructuring is to move from a 19th century factory model to a more personalized design that better reflects the current needs of all children for this new millennium.

WHAT COURSES DO YOU NEED TO TAKE?

The traditional "education as a major" or "bachelor's degree in education" is quickly disappearing. Accreditation agencies would rather you have a liberal arts major (elementary) or an academic major (secondary and postsecondary) first, followed by professional education preparation. In some states, the professional education courses are a fifth-year program that may not begin in your senior year. Professional education courses include education theory, courses in pedagogy, and practical field experiences.

E.C.E. (EARLY CHILDHOOD EDUCATION). The trend is toward a major in early childhood education, which includes courses and experiences in professional early childhood and preschool education.

ELEMENTARY ED. (GRADES K–6). The trend is toward a liberal studies major leading to a bachelor's degree, followed by professional education experiences, which include student teaching for one or more semesters at an elementary school.

MIDDLE LEVEL ED. (GRADES 5–8). The trend is toward an academic major leading to a bachelor's degree (e.g., in English, biology, mathematics, history, etc.) followed by the professional education experiences, including student teaching at a middle school.

SECONDARY ED. (GRADES 7–12). The trend is toward an academic major leading to a bachelor's degree followed by the professional education experiences, including student teaching at the high school level.

COMMUNITY COLLEGE (TWO-YEAR). The requirements vary considerably because of the diversity of the community college mission. For academic fields in the transfer program (preparing students for transfer to a four-year program), a master's degree in the subject you teach is the minimum requirement. Only about half of the programs in community colleges are in the transfer area. Vocational education (in such areas as business, real estate, and traffic safety, designed to prepare or update students for careers) usually requires a bachelor's degree plus work experience in the field.

COLLEGE AND UNIVERSITY (FOUR-YEAR). The usual minimum requirement for full-time tenure-track employment is a doctoral degree in the field.

WHAT CAN YOU DO WITH A DEGREE IN EDUCATION?

The obvious answer: TEACH! And the good news is that there is a big demand for teachers as we approach the year 2000. Because of the graying of today's faculties and the growth of the country's population, the projected need for teachers at all levels will be great for the next decade. Preparation for a career in education prepares you to meet the challenges that have always faced education. Because of their dissatisfaction with formal education for the past half-century, Americans are in a process of inquiry, self-reflection, and change. Education is a reflection of this change. As a teacher, you will undoubtedly be a part of the changes.

WHAT DO EXPERTS SAY ABOUT EDUCATION?

Dr. Richard Kellough, Education Professor at California State University in Sacramento, offers this advice to prospective students:

What can a person expect during the course of study? Students should expect to do a lot of field work in public school. They'll either be student teaching or participating in some other way, but they'll be interacting with the students in the classroom.

What are the characteristics of a successful student? They have to really like children and enjoy working with them. This is true for all ages, from 5 to 17. They also need "people" skills when working with adults. Many successful students in education are dedicated to getting good grades in school. They can identify and solve problems.

What do you see for the future of the discipline? There will be much more interaction with others in the future and not so many isolated classrooms. Teachers will work together and there will be a greater attempt to involve parents. There will be a need for teachers at all levels in the future—there are not enough people getting the needed degrees to fill the demand.

What makes this field exciting to you, personally, and why do you love what you do? There is no better time to be a teacher. People are working together, solving problems and preparing others to meet the world. The standards are high and the training is rigorous, which will lead us to excellence.

BEFORE YOU DECIDE . . .

Before you invest the next four years pursuing this field of study, invest a few hours in a thorough investigation of what a degree in education can do for you. Use the following suggestions and the worksheet at the end of this chapter to make a plan for conducting some field research. Once your plan is complete and approved by your instructor, proceed to Part 5, Field Research, where you'll find further instructions for making the most of these activities.

TALK ABOUT IT

Conduct interviews with the following three people (using the information included in the Field Research section in Part 5 of this book to guide your discussions):

- A senior completing a major in education
- An education professor at your school
- A professional working in an education-related career

READ ABOUT IT

Following is a book listing that provides an overview of possible career options for someone with a degree in education.

- Anthony, Rebecca. *Educator's Passport to International Jobs*. Princeton, NJ: Peterson's, 1984.
- Anthony, Rebecca and Gerald Roe. *From Contact to Contract: A Teacher's Employment Guide*. New York: Sulzburger & Graham, 1994.
- *Careers in Teaching Handbook*. Belmont, MA: Recruiting New Teachers, 1993.
- Edelfelt, Roy. *Careers in Education*. Lincolnwood, IL: VGM Career Horizons, 1993.
- Eberts, Marjorie and Margaret Gisler. *Careers for Kids at Heart*. Lincolnwood, IL: VGM Career Horizons, 1994.
- Fine, Janet. *Opportunities in Teaching Careers*. Lincolnwood, IL: VGM Career Horizons, 1995.
- Krannich, Ronald. *Educator's Guide to Alternative Jobs and Careers*. Manassas, VA: Impact Publications, 1991.
- Levin, Joel. *How to Get a Job in Education*. Holbrook, MA: Adams Media Corp., 1995.
- Plevin, Arlene. *Education as a Career*. Washington, D.C.: National Education Association, 1988.
- Pollack, Sandy. *Alternative Careers for Teachers*. Boston: Harvard Common Press, 1984.

EXPERIENCE IT

Seek out an opportunity to see what a degree in education can do for you in the workplace. Arrange a tour, a job-shadowing experience, or even a full-fledged internship at a place such as:

- A child care center
- An elementary school
- A high school
- A middle school
- A school or class for special needs children
- A county or state level education administration office
- A nursing home for elderly people
- A textbook publishing house

Once you have scheduled a first appointment, use the information included in the Field Research section of this book to make the most of this experience.

EXPLORE THE OPTIONS

Using the materials included in the Field Research section at the end of this book, conduct a thorough investigation of at least two career options for college graduates with an education degree. You'll need a good selection of career books and resources and access to the Internet to complete this task. Here are some ways to put a degree in education to work. Use this list for ideas but feel free to focus your exploration on another idea that interests you.

- College Administrator
- College Professor
- Corporate Trainer
- Counselor
- Early Childhood Education Professional
- Educational Consultant
- Elementary School Administrator
- High School Teacher
- Librarian
- Middle School Teacher
- Public Administrator
- Special Education Teacher
- Speech/Language Pathologist
- Teacher (K–12)
- Vocational and Adult Education Teacher

REFERENCE

Kellough, Richard and E. Roberts. *Resource Guide for Elementary School Teaching*. Upper Saddle River, NJ: Prentice Hall, 1997.

Now that you've learned a little about what a major in education is like, think about what it means for you. Could this be a good choice? Can you say with reasonable certainty that it's not a good fit at all? Use the following planning worksheet to explain your response.

NO WAY!

Here are three reasons why I don't think this major would be a good choice for me.

_____

_____

_____

Stop! If you are sure this is not a major you want to pursue, don't waste another minute! Move on and explore another major.

A DEFINITE MAYBE

Here are three reasons why I think this major might be a good choice for me.

_____

_____

_____

Following are my plans to find out all I can about this major.

FIELD RESEARCH PROJECT 1: TALK ABOUT IT

I will use materials included in the Field Research section of this book (Part 5) to conduct interviews with the following people:

_____ Senior completing a major in education

_____ Education professor

_____ Education professional

FIELD RESEARCH PROJECT 2: READ ABOUT IT

I will use the materials included in Part 5 of this book to review the following book(s) about potential career tracks:

_____

_____

Field Research Worksheet

FIELD RESEARCH PROJECT 3: EXPERIENCE IT

I have arranged a tour or job-shadowing experience at the following location and will use the materials included in Part 5 of this book to record my observations:

_____ Location

_____ Contact Person

_____ Date and Time of Appointment

FIELD RESEARCH PROJECT 4: EXPLORE THE OPTIONS

I want to find out all I can about the following career(s) and will use the materials included in Part 5 of this book to guide my investigation at the library and on the Internet:

_____ Career Choice #1

_____ Career Choice #2

_____

Student's Name and Date

_____ Field Research Plan Approved

_____ Field Research Plan Not Approved

Because:

_____

_____

_____

Instructor's Signature and Date

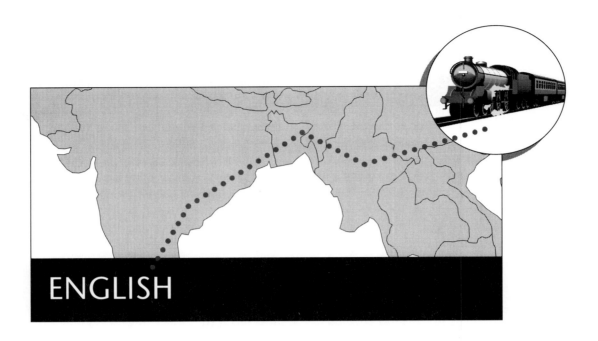

ENGLISH

Is This Major for You?

- Are you a crossword puzzle junkie, easily enthralled with the search for the perfect word?
- Do you sometimes find yourself mentally editing newscasts and correcting the grammar of other people?
- Are you a news junkie—watching every newscast and reading every newspaper that you can?
- Do people often compliment you on your great vocabulary?
- Are essay questions your favorite kind of test question (face it, you can talk or write your way through anything)?
- Do you keep a journal, write great letters, and wind up helping all of your friends with their research papers?
- Have you got a track record of active participation on your school yearbook and/or newspaper staffs?
- Do you spend a lot of your spare time with your nose in a good book?
- Do you often find titles of some of your all-time favorite books on your "English Lit" teacher's recommended reading lists?
- Can you spot a typographical or grammatical error a mile away?

If you answered yes to several of these questions, keep reading and find out if an English major is a good choice for you.

Dr. W.T. Pfefferle, English Professor at Texas Wesleyan University, contributed to this article.

INTRODUCTION

English is the language by which most of us communicate and express ourselves. On a personal level, English allows us to convey what we think, feel, and want. In the larger picture, it allows us to conduct business, educate ourselves, and teach others. Globally, English is the native language of over 400 million people, the largest language community except Mandarin Chinese. It is spoken in nearly every country of the world and is the predominant language on two of the six inhabited continents. It is the second language of millions of Europeans and Asians and is the official language of more than a dozen countries. English is the closest thing to a world language that has ever existed!

WHAT IS ENGLISH?

The study of English as a major discipline is composed of two different areas of concentration: literature and composition and writing. Literature explores the fiction, drama, and poetry of different cultures. It involves criticism of the literature being studied. Literature majors can study writings from a number of different time periods and cultures or can concentrate on a broad, deep understanding of just one area, such as Renaissance poetry or 20th-century French novels. Literature can be studied as a source of psychological and social insight as well as an art.

Composition and writing deals with the mechanics of language, the structure of types of compositions, grammar, rhetoric (theory behind the composition), and creative writing. Courses in these areas deal not only with subjects but with how to teach them.

HISTORY AND BACKGROUND

Language is the very core of society. The ancient Greeks and Romans studied the nature and origins of languages and developed strong theories of rhetoric, or how language could be used to benefit society. They emphasized the importance of language structure as an effective communication tool. How can language best be used to accomplish the ends we desire? During all of history, people have used language in poetry, drama, short stories, and novels to express themselves and their messages.

The earliest literature came from the Middle East about 3000 B.C. and included fables, epics, histories, hymns, love songs, and philosophical essays. The poems of Homer, the dramas of Sophocles, and the philosophical writings of Aristotle greatly influenced the development of Western civilization. Later, the writings and speeches of Cicero and Julius Caesar give us a clear idea about Roman civilization.

During the Middle Ages, epic poems such as *Beowulf* recorded legends that had previously been preserved by word of mouth. Narrative stories of adventure, fantasy, and knightly honor began to appear. Wandering minstrels composed songs to entertain the lords and ladies of the courts. The writings of Geoffrey

Chaucer solidified the form of our present English language, and he became known as the "Father of English Poetry."

The Renaissance scholars (1300s–1500s) rediscovered the Greek and Roman classics and were the first to study ancient literature. In England, the Renaissance produced some of the finest literature in the English language. Though there were many excellent writers of the period, William Shakespeare's works exemplified the achievements of the age. Other periods of literature followed:

CLASSICISM (1600–1700). Also called the Age of Reason, classic writers depicted an idealized life as more rational and orderly than it is. Thomas Hobbes, John Locke, and Sir Isaac Newton wrote during this time.

ROMANTICISM (MID-1700s TO MID-1800s). In contrast to the classicists, the romantics emphasized passion and imagination over reason and logic. Nathaniel Hawthorne, Edgar Allan Poe, and James Fenimore Cooper are among the romantic writers.

REALISM (MID-1800s TO THE PRESENT). This approach to writing seeks to present life as objectively as possible without the distortion caused by the writer's feelings. Realists offer ordinary characters in ordinary situations. Early realists include Jane Austen, Charles Dickens, Henry James, Mark Twain, and Sinclair Lewis.

By the 20th century, writers were expanding these approaches and experimenting with form and technique to create new voices for their thoughts. Their works reflect the social and political conditions of the times. Ernest Hemingway, F. Scott Fitzgerald, and Eugene O'Neill are among the many influential writers of this century.

ENGLISH TODAY

Today, we live in an information age where communication is frequent and immediate. Everything is influenced by language ability. Effective writing and speaking in business, the media, and the culture are essential to progress. The ancient Greek idea that it's not what you say, but how you say it applies today perhaps more than ever before when we consider the sheer volume of written and verbal language that surrounds us. Individuals with an understanding of English and how to use it effectively can contribute to every aspect of our society.

WHAT COURSES DO YOU NEED TO TAKE?

Typical requirements and electives for a B. A. in English are as follows:

LITERATURE MAJOR

Contemporary World Literature	History of English Novel
Critical Writing	History of the English Language
English Renaissance Literature	Intro to Literary Studies
English Romanticism	Medieval Literature
History of American Literature	Shakespeare
History of British Drama	20th Century Fiction

There are two ways to approach a literature major. You can become a generalist, taking a wide variety of courses to become well-rounded in the field of literature, or you can specialize in one segment of the literary spectrum, for example, African American fiction or Chaucer. The trend is toward a broad approach since specialization narrows your marketability.

COMPOSITION MAJOR

Advanced Composition	Technical Writing
Creative Writing	Topics in Rhetoric
Intro to Literary Studies	Topics in Writing
Teaching Composition	Writing Project

Skills in computer technology are essential for the English major today, as many career paths increasingly require competence in this area.

WHAT CAN YOU DO WITH A DEGREE IN ENGLISH?

Many who major in English also have a degree in education and plan to teach, but an English major is also excellent preparation for careers in the legal profession, business administration and management, mass communication, journalism, and advertising and public relations. Careers in journalism include writing, editing, and publishing. Designing your undergraduate degree program to include courses to target other areas increases your marketability in business employment.

Future employment is an important thing for English majors to think about before embarking on their course of study. Many students look upon an English major as the background for a career writing novels and stories. While some realize this goal, many do not, and they are left without means to support themselves when their material does not sell. Some English majors find teaching positions in their areas of expertise (a certain literary period, for example) but have not acquired the teaching experience and background to be effective in the classroom. Neither they nor their students benefit from this situation. Don't abandon dreams of literary greatness—dreams do come true! Just be practical in the approach you take to your education so that your skills won't be wasted for lack of employment marketability. Society needs you!

WHAT DO EXPERTS SAY ABOUT ENGLISH?

Dr. W.T. Pfefferle, English Professor at Texas Wesleyan Univeristy, offers this advice to prospective students:

What can a person expect during the course of study? I think, typically, English majors find that they are asked to write more than they imagine. English majors tend to understand reading will be a part of their discipline, but the amount of critical thinking and writing that they are asked to do often exceeds their expectations.

What are the characteristics of a good student? A good student has good work habits, a creative mind, and a tenacious attitude. Being a bit of a dreamer always helps too, as long as the dreamer is able to rein in those flights of fancy.

What do you see for the future of the discipline? The ongoing split between literature and composition is a challenge. These are actually very different disciplines and necessarily should be separated in every possible way.

What makes this field exciting to you, personally, and why do you love what you do? I am passionate about English because of my students. I love watching developing minds figure things out. I see little "lightbulbs" go off in brains every semester. I chose the discipline because I had good English instructors. I saw the satisfaction they found and wanted it for myself.

BEFORE YOU DECIDE . . .

Before you invest the next four years pursuing this field of study, invest a few hours in a thorough investigation of what a degree in English can do for you. Use the following suggestions and the worksheet at the end of this chapter to make a plan for conducting some field research. Once your plan is complete and approved by your instructor, proceed to the Field Research chapter at the end of the book where you'll find further instructions for making the most of these activities.

TALK ABOUT IT

Conduct interviews with the following three people (using the information included in the Field Research section of this book to guide your discussions):

- A senior completing a major in English
- An English professor at your school
- A professional working in an English-related field

READ ABOUT IT

Following is a book listing that provides an overview of possible career options for someone with a degree in English.

- Bly, Robert. *Careers for Writers and Others Who Have a Way With Words*. Lincolnwood, IL: VGM Career Horizons, 1996.
- DeGalan, Julie. *Great Jobs for English Majors*. Lincolnwood, IL: VGM Career Horizons, 1996.
- Eberts, Marjorie and Margaret Gisler. *Careers for Bookworms and Other Literary Types*. Lincolnwood, IL: VGM Career Horizons, 1996.
- Field, Shelley. *100 Best Careers for Writers and Artists*. New York: Macmillan Publishing, 1998.
- Goldberg, Jan. *Careers in Journalism*. Lincolnwood, IL: VGM Career Horizons, 1995.
- Guilley, Rosemary Ellen. *Career Opportunities for Writers*. New York: Facts On File, 1995.
- Meyer, Scott A. *100 Jobs in Words*. New York: Macmillan, 1996.
- Morgan, Bradley J. *Book Publishing Career Directory*. Detroit: Visible Ink Press, 1993.

- Morgan, Bradley J. *Magazine Publishing Career Directory*. Detroit: Visible Ink Press, 1993.
- Munschauer, John L. *Jobs for English Majors and Other Smart People*. Princeton, NJ: Peterson's, 1991.
- Pattis, S. William and Robert A. Carter. *Opportunities in Publishing Careers*. Lincolnwood, IL: VGM Career Horizons, 1995.

EXPERIENCE IT

Seek out an opportunity to see what a degree in English might do for you in the workplace. Arrange a tour, a job-shadowing experience, or even a full-fledged internship at a place such as:

- A newspaper, magazine, or book publisher
- A local bookstore or library
- An advertising agency or public relations firm
- The publications department of a corporation or nonprofit agency

EXPLORE THE OPTIONS

Using the materials included in the Field Research section at the end of this book, conduct a thorough investigation of at least two career options for college graduates with an English degree. You'll need a good selection of career books and resources and access to the Internet to complete this task. Here are some ways to put a degree in English to work. Use this list for ideas but feel free to focus your exploration on another idea that interests you.

- Abstractor
- Advertising Executive
- Archivist
- Author
- Book Designer
- Cartoonist
- CD-ROM Designer
- Communications Consultant
- Copywriter
- Correspondent
- Curriculum Designer
- Development Director
- Editor
- English Teacher
- Freelance Writer
- Indexer
- Information Broker
- Journalist
- Librarian
- Literary Agent
- Marketing Specialist
- Paralegal
- Press Secretary
- Proofreader
- Public Information Officer
- Publicist
- Publisher

REFERENCE

Pfefferle, W.T. *Writing That Matters*. Upper Saddle River, NJ: Prentice Hall, 1998.

Now that you've learned a little about what a major in English is like, think about what it means for you. Could this be a good choice? Can you say with reasonable certainty that it's not a good fit at all? Use the following planning worksheet to explain your response.

NO WAY!

Here are three reasons why I don't think this major would be a good choice for me.

_____

_____

_____

Stop! If you are sure this is not a major you want to pursue, don't waste another minute! Move on and explore another major.

A DEFINITE MAYBE

Here are three reasons why I think this major might be a good choice for me.

_____

_____

_____

Following are my plans to find out all I can about this major.

FIELD RESEARCH PROJECT 1: TALK ABOUT IT

I will use the materials included in the Field Research section of this book (Part 5) to conduct interviews with the following people:

_____ Senior completing a major in English

_____ English professor

_____ English professional

FIELD RESEARCH PROJECT 2: READ ABOUT IT

I will use the materials included in Part 5 of this book to review the following book(s) about potential career tracks:

_____

_____

FIELD RESEARCH PROJECT 3: EXPERIENCE IT

I have arranged a tour or job-shadowing experience at the following location and will use the materials included in Part 5 of this book to record my observations:

_____ Location

_____ Contact Person

_____ Date and Time of Appointment

FIELD RESEARCH PROJECT 4: EXPLORE THE OPTIONS

I want to find out all I can about the following career(s) and will use the materials included in Part 5 of this book to guide my investigation at the library and on the Internet:

_____ Career Choice #1

_____ Career Choice #2

· ·

_____

Student's Name and Date

_____ Field Research Plan Approved

_____ Field Research Plan Not Approved

Because:

_____

_____

_____

Instructor's Signature and Date

· ·

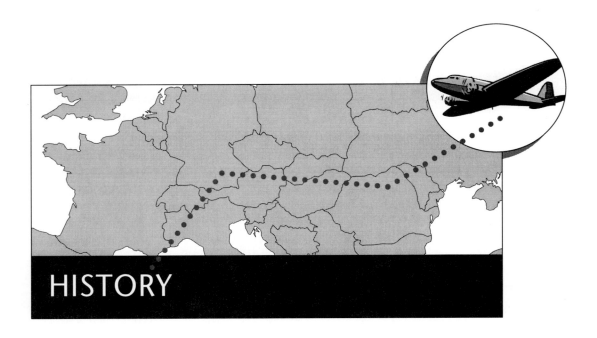

HISTORY

Is This Major for You?

- Do you have a fascination with the people, places, events, and ideas of the past?
- Can you formulate a good argument for an issue you care about?
- Can you apply lessons from the past to current situations?
- Can you effectively distinguish between relevant and irrelevant information?
- Do you enjoy working with information?
- Is reading a favorite pastime of yours (with biographies at the top of your list)?
- Are research projects among your favorite type of course assignment?

If you answered yes to several of these questions, keep reading to find out if a major in history is a good choice for you.

INTRODUCTION

A great historian once said, "Everyone knows what history is until he begins to think about it. After that, nobody knows." If we think of history as everything that ever happened, it would include all the changes in the universe since the beginning of time. More practically, history can be viewed from two perspectives: the events of the past that make up the human experience on earth and the written record of those events. Beyond the chronology that lets us see how the world came to be, history provides crucial insight into present human behavior. The past has shaped people and forces that influence us today.

Dr. David Goldfield, History Professor at University of North Carolina, contributed to this article.

HISTORY AND BACKGROUND

Scientists estimate that Earth is six billion years old. Human creatures began to appear one to two million years ago, with homo sapiens emerging about 200,000 years ago. The earliest remains of modern humans date from about 90,000 years ago. Civilization as we know it emerged around 3000 B.C. Humans, as cultural creatures, have built ways of living in a group that are passed from generation to generation. Human behavior, language, and biological and sociological adaptation have made possible the spread of humanity to nearly every land on Earth.

Emerson once said that history may be resolved into the biographies of a few great men. Many 19th century historians agreed that leaders of the past simply did what they had to do depending upon the social and economic circumstances of their times. Did the circumstances cause leaders to act, or did their actions create the circumstances? Most historians today agree that it is a combination of the two. The history of most nations includes many eras: dark ages, renaissances, revolutions, invasions, times of prosperity, and centuries of decay. Greece and Italy have ancient ruins, impressive monuments to their civilizations. The story of the United States, however, is brief and continuous, with comparatively little violence occurring on native soil. We are not a land of ruins, and our history has played a vital role in shaping the circumstances of the world today.

An important aspect of history is the content. History is made not so much by the people who live it as by the people who write about it and the way in which they tell the story. Historians write about subjects that reflect the interests, tastes, and purposes of the times in which they write, and they naturally use the language that mirrors popular sentiment. Many argue that until the latter half of the 1900s, history was primarily written from a white, male point of view, leaving the perspectives and contributions of women and minorities to a less prominent role, if recorded at all. Others argue that because society was largely driven by white males that historians were reflecting the interests and purposes of the times. A heated debate exists about whether or not "rewriting history" to accommodate a more diverse perspective will change how we understand the past.

HISTORY TODAY

Historians today are in an excellent position to relate our past with our present in a rapidly changing world and economy. In this country, history is increasingly popular with the general public as we examine American ideals and the way conflict between those ideals and reality has shaped the nation's development. This conflict has broadened the understanding and application of American ideals to include formerly excluded people. This is not to say that American history is a heroic tale of constant improvement—many conflicts about the meaning of our ideals have been resolved only after great struggle and pain. The United States is a diverse nation not always comfortable with that diversity. Yet when we look to our history—particularly our Declaration of Independence—we find ideals that set a higher standard than we might otherwise set for ourselves. Striving to maintain these ideals is important now more than ever before. Historians are in a position to help us gain a perspective on where we have been, where we are, and where we are going.

WHAT COURSES DO YOU NEED TO TAKE?

Following are typical course requirements for a major in history:

African History	Statistics
Asian Civilization	United States History
Research Methods	World History

Courses in written and oral communication, and quantitative and qualitative research analysis are also important assets for history majors.

WHAT CAN YOU DO WITH A DEGREE IN HISTORY?

History majors can use their communications, synthesis, and interpretive skills in today's workplace. They can take advantage of advances in electronic communication and the globalization of the economy because they are taught to think beyond disciplinary boundaries and to communicate through a diversity of venues. Careers include archivists, catalogers, customs inspectors, genealogists, museum curators, and teachers. There are opportunities with publishing houses and positions as sales representatives, advertising copywriters, public relations officers, foreign service officers, journalists and correspondents, and attorneys.

History is an ideal undergraduate major for law and medicine because it emphasizes the essential intellectual skills: critical thinking, research, writing and speaking. Historians know how to analyze problems, understand society, and communicate effectively.

WHAT DO EXPERTS SAY ABOUT HISTORY?

Dr. David Goldfield, History Professor at University of North Carolina, offers this advice to prospective students:

What can a person expect during the course of study? Students can expect to learn three basic skills in college. First they learn to communicate using written, oral, and electronic media. Second, by conducting research, students learn to synthesize large amounts of quantitative and qualitative data, analyze the material, and interpret it for a wider audience. They will undertake studies that teach them to think beyond the boundaries of history.

What are the characteristics of a successful student? The successful student enjoys looking at problems from many different perspectives, and is a bit of a detective about making the past both whole and alive.

What do you see for the future of the discipline? The future of the discipline is rapidly changing as history is written and taught by historians who tend to diminish the importance of bringing disparate pieces of the past together into a coherent whole. This fragments historical perspectives. Some of the fragmentation is good in that it has given a voice to groups and events previously omitted from the American story, but we need to remember to retain both sense and order in the discipline without sacrificing the positive advances we have made in historical research in the past decade.

BEFORE YOU DECIDE . . .

Before you invest the next four years pursuing this field of study, invest a few hours in a thorough investigation of what a degree in history can do for you. Use the following suggestions and the worksheet at the end of this chapter to make a plan for conducting some field research. Once your plan is complete and approved by your instructor, proceed to Part 5, Field Research, where you'll find further instructions for making the most of these activities.

TALK ABOUT IT

Conduct interviews with the following three people (using the information included in the Field Research section in Part 5 of this book to guide your discussions):

- A senior completing a major in history
- A history professor at your school
- A professional working in a history-related career

READ ABOUT IT

Following is a book listing that provides an overview of possible career options for someone with a degree in history.

- Camenson, Blythe. *Careers for History Buffs and Others Who Learn from the Past.* Lincolnwood, IL: VGM Career Horizons, 1994.
- Camenson, Blythe. *Careers for Mystery Buffs and Other Snoops and Sleuths.* Lincolnwood, IL: VGM Career Horizons, 1997.
- DeGalan, Julie and Stephen Lambert. *Great Jobs for History Majors.* Lincolnwood, IL: VGM Career Horizons, 1995.
- Howe, Barbara J. *Career Choices for Students of History.* New York: Walker, 1990.

EXPERIENCE IT

Seek out an opportunity to see what a degree in history can do for you in the workplace. Arrange a tour, a job-shadowing experience, or even a full-fledged internship at a place such as:

- A museum administrative office
- The preservation department of a historical landmark
- The United Nations or a foreign embassy
- An investigative bureau
- A law firm or courthouse
- The legal affairs department of a corporation
- An educational publishing company

Once you have scheduled a first appointment, use the information included in the Field Research section of this book to make the most of this experience.

EXPLORE THE OPTIONS

Using the materials included in the Field Research section at the end of this book, conduct a thorough investigation of at least two career options for college graduates with a history degree. You'll need a good selection of career books and resources and access to the Internet to complete this task. Here are some ways to put a degree in history to work. Use this list for ideas but feel free to focus your exploration on another idea that interests you.

- Anthropologist
- Archivist
- Cataloger
- College Professor
- Customs Inspector
- Diplomat
- Editor
- Foreign Correspondent
- Foreign Service Officer
- Genealogist
- Historian
- Historical Preservation Officer
- Investigator
- Journalist
- Lawyer
- Librarian
- Living History Museum Director
- Lobbyist
- Military Officer
- Museum Curator
- Paralegal
- Policy Analyst
- Political Scientist
- Politician
- Public Administrator
- Publisher
- Researcher
- Teacher (K–12)
- Textbook Writer

REFERENCE

Goldfield, David, Carl Abbott, Virginia DeJohn Anderson, Peter H. Argersinger, William L. Barney, and Robert M. Weir. *The American Journey: A History of the United States.* Upper Saddle River, NJ: Prentice Hall, 1997.

Field Research Worksheet

Now that you've learned a little about what a major in history is like, think about what it means for you. Could this be a good choice for you? Can you say with reasonable certainty that it's not a good fit at all? Use the following planning worksheet to explain your response.

NO WAY!

Here are three reasons why I don't think this major would be a good choice for me.

_____

_____

_____

Stop! If you are sure this is not a major you want to pursue, don't waste another minute! Move on and explore another major.

A DEFINITE MAYBE

Here are three reasons why I think this major might be a good choice for me.

_____

_____

_____

Following are my plans to find out all I can about this major.

FIELD RESEARCH PROJECT 1: TALK ABOUT IT

I will use the materials included in the Field Research section of this book (Part 5) to conduct interviews with the following people:

_____ Senior completing a major in history

_____ History professor

_____ History professional

FIELD RESEARCH PROJECT 2: READ ABOUT IT

I will use the materials included in Part 5 of this book to review the following book(s) about potential career tracks:

_____

_____

FIELD RESEARCH PROJECT 3: EXPERIENCE IT

I have arranged a tour or job-shadowing experience at the following location and will use the materials included in Part 5 of this book to record my observations:

_____ Location

_____ Contact Person

_____ Date and Time of Appointment

FIELD RESEARCH PROJECT 4: EXPLORE THE OPTIONS

I want to find out all I can about the following career(s) and will use the materials included in Part 5 of this book to guide my investigation at the library and on the Internet:

_____ Career Choice #1

_____ Career Choice #2

_____

Student's Name and Date

_____ Field Research Plan Approved

_____ Field Research Plan Not Approved

Because:

_____

_____

_____

Instructor's Signature and Date

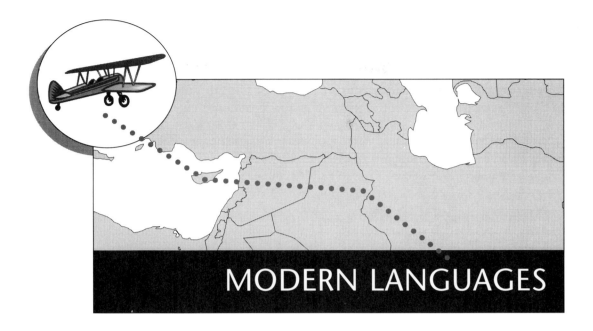

MODERN LANGUAGES

Is This Major for You?

- Do you speak more than one language at least semi-fluently?
- Are you intrigued by the customs and cultures of other countries?
- Do you enjoy traveling to new places?
- Are you always game to try different types of exotic cuisine?
- Have you spent time in another country—either as a tourist, an exchange student, or otherwise?
- Are you interested in world affairs?

If you answered yes to several of these questions, keep reading and find out if a major in modern languages is a good choice for you.

INTRODUCTION

At a small liberal arts university in North Carolina, an undergraduate student majoring in French works her way through school working for McDonald's. This is not an unusual story at first glance. Upon graduation, however, this student markets her experience and skill in French and management, goes to work for McDonald's in France, and soon becomes head of the corporation's French operation. She is so successful that McDonald's capitalizes on her language competence, teaches her to speak Portuguese, and she is now the head of McDonald's operation in Portugal. Modern languages skills are becoming increasingly valued in the international business market, and if you have the talent and discipline to master a language, this important field may be for you.

Dr. Cathy Pons, Professor at University of North Carolina at Asheville, contributed to this article.

WHAT IS A MODERN LANGUAGE?

Traditionally, a foreign language major meant the study of the literature of a country and its language. The focus now is not limited to a particular time and place. Rather, language study today encompasses the literature, culture, and media of the people who use a given language. It includes understanding the socioeconomic, political, and educational systems of a particular language group. Modern language study also encompasses linguistics, the understanding of language as a system, and how the language is used in varying social contexts. Major languages considered in modern language study today are French, Spanish, German, English, Russian, Chinese, and Japanese.

HISTORY AND BACKGROUND

The word *language* comes from the Latin word *lingua*, meaning tongue, and human speech and writing makes it possible for people to communicate. People learn their native language automatically by listening and imitating the language of their environment. For children, all languages are equally easy to learn by the natural speaking method (listening and imitating). Older students learn foreign languages by learning grammar (the rules of the language) in the classroom and through spoken language by imitating sounds, words, and sentences and by using the language in a practical setting, in conversation, and by linking with foreign cultures on the Internet.

In the ancient world, Latin became the language of the rulers as the conquests of Rome covered the civilized western world. Latin influenced the languages of the common people, but each local group developed its own dialect. Later, when universities were organized in the west, they offered study in languages, but most literature and other subjects remained in Latin. The invention of the printing press in the mid-1400s allowed books to be produced in the languages of the people. Latin began to be replaced as national languages strengthened. Sooner or later, governing bodies of various countries had to declare an official language for conducting business and communication. For example, what we know as French today is just one of the many regional dialects that existed in France in the Middle Ages.

Ancient Greeks and Romans studied the nature and origins of language but lacked scientific methodology in their studies. The scientific study of language began in the late 1700s and continues today with linguistics, the study of languages as systems of patterns, sounds, and rules. Linguistical study today includes sociolinguistics, applied linguistics, and second language acquisition.

MODERN LANGUAGES TODAY

The study of foreign languages today is increasingly an interdisciplinary endeavor. It includes the various perspectives—economics, sociology, politics—of the many cultures where a given language is spoken. For example, French is spoken as an official language in Europe, Canada, Louisiana (in the U.S.), Haiti, and many countries in Africa. To study the language in the context of France alone is to omit the rich cultural context of the language on a global scale. There is an emphasis today on helping students develop real-life proficiencies in language usage in addition to knowing its literature.

There is also an emphasis on integrating the study of linguistics into foreign language programs. This helps students analyze a language as a system and understand how and why the native speakers use the constructions they do. Language and culture are inseparable, and language is always changing. It is influenced by historical events and social circumstances. Students gain a real-life perspective for using a language by looking at how it reflects the culture. This is particularly important as businesses and organizations become increasingly internationalized and global communication becomes a way of life.

Because children learn languages more readily at a young age, the current trend in education is to offer foreign languages in elementary and middle schools. This gives students the basis for further study of a particular language, which makes it easier to learn other foreign languages. Research has indicated that language study increases reading comprehension, critical thinking skills, and vocabulary in other areas of study.

WHAT COURSES DO YOU NEED TO TAKE?

Most high schools today offer modern languages, and most college programs expect that you come to them with at least a basic knowledge of the language you want to pursue. Students who have three to four years of high school language study immediately begin language skill courses such as writing, oral skills (listening and speaking), and surveys of literature and civilization. Other course work, in addition to the core courses of the program you select, include overviews of the history of the language, composition, film, and areas of interdisciplinary study, to connect your chosen language to a business or education context and study abroad.

Modern language study is increasing its integration with technology, a logical combination. Software programs, CD ROMS, and the Internet provide many ways to practice language skills and experience new cultures. Following are the kinds of courses and electives that most programs include (for the purposes of these examples, French will be used in the course titles, but this course overview applies to modern languages in general):

Composition and Structural Review Survey of French Civilization and Literature	Intermediate French
	Masters of French Film
	Oral Skills
Francophone Studies	Studies in French Civilization
French Phonetics	Studies in French Literature
French View of America	The French Language
History of French Cinema	

WHAT CAN YOU DO WITH A DEGREE IN MODERN LANGUAGES?

You can combine your language major with teacher certification for K–12 education (teaching at the postsecondary level generally requires an advanced degree). With global technology, business is becoming ever more international in scope. This offers many opportunities to individuals with competence in foreign languages, both in the business itself and in international relations. The need to communicate across cultures has increased the need for interpreters and translators in both the public and private sectors. International travel offers opportunities as flight attendants, travel agents, and tour guides. Technology fields need audio-visual specialists, computer programmers, and software designers.

WHAT DO EXPERTS SAY ABOUT MODERN LANGUAGES?

Dr. Cathy Pons, Professor at the University of North Carolina at Asheville, offers this advice to prospective students:

What can a person expect during the course of study? A student studying foreign languages today needs to be open to new ideas and perspectives. There are many similarities in Northern European cultures, yet there are differences as well. Students need to guard against stereotypes and measuring cultural phenomena against their own culture. Students will gain a new perspective of their own culture by understanding another cultural perspective. In a world where diversity is the rule, we need to develop our skills to get along with others.

What are the characteristics of a successful student? A successful student is one who is willing to take risks and have the self-confidence to be uncomfortable. In learning a language, you have to be willing to sound and act like someone from the culture you are learning about, to act like someone besides yourself. You need to be disciplined to work regularly. If you get behind in the study, you can't read a lot more some evening to make up for it. Language is not only about knowledge, it's about skill. You need to practice on a daily basis if you want to succeed.

What do you see for the future of the discipline? The discipline is becoming more and more interdisciplinary in nature as we make links between language and culture, language and business. People are taking the study of foreign language more seriously, starting it earlier in schools. Remaining competitive in today's global economy requires that we make some changes in education and place more emphasis on how we will meet the demands of international commerce.

What makes this field exciting to you, personally, and why do you love what you do? The field is exciting to me because I love the applied aspects—how people use language, how they acquire it, and convey meaning with it. Sociolinguistics has only been a recognized field for the past 20 or 30 years. Using this discipline, we try to get into the head of the other person, to try on another identity in order to understand and better communicate. The field of languages is broadening. Whatever a person's interest, she can find a way to relate it to language study.

BEFORE YOU DECIDE . . .

Before you invest the next four years pursuing this field of study, invest a few hours in a thorough investigation of what a degree in modern languages can do for you. Use the following suggestions and the worksheet at the end of this chapter to make a plan for conducting some field research. Once your plan is complete and approved by your instructor, proceed to Part 5, Field Research, where you'll find further instructions for making the most of these activities.

TALK ABOUT IT

Conduct interviews with the following three people (using the information included in the Field Research section in Part 5 of this book to guide your discussions):

- A senior completing a degree in modern language
- A modern language professor at your school
- A professional working in a modern language-related career

READ ABOUT IT

Following is a book listing that provides an overview of possible career options for someone with a degree in modern language.

- Arnold, Edwin. *Foreign Language Careers*. Lincolnwood, IL: NTC Publishing, 1995.
- Arpan, Jeffery. *Opportunities in International Business*. Lincolnwood, IL: NTC Publishing, 1995.
- Bouigain, Edward. *Foreign Language and Your Career*. New York: Guilford, 1993.
- Halloran, Edward J. *Careers in International Business*. Lincolnwood, IL: VGM Career Horizons, 1996.
- Kocher, Eric. *International Jobs: Where They Are and How to Get Them*. New York: Addison Wesley, 1993.
- Rivers, Wilga A. *Opportunities in Foreign Language Careers*. Lincolnwood, IL: VGM Career Horizons, 1995.
- Seelye, H. Ned and Lawrence J. Day. *Careers for Foreign Language Aficionados and Other Multilingual Types*. 1995.
- Shorto, Russell. *Careers for Foreign Language Experts*. New York: Houghton Mifflin, 1992.

EXPERIENCE IT

Seek out an opportunity to see what a degree in modern languages can do for you in the workplace. Arrange a tour, a job-shadowing experience, or even a full-fledged internship at a place such as:

- A foreign embassy
- A U.S. customs office
- A worldwide tour company
- A cruise line ship
- A U.S. corporation doing business internationally
- A foreign corporation doing business in the U.S.
- A publisher who translates books into other languages

Once you have scheduled a first appointment, use the information included in the Field Research section of this book to make the most of this experience.

EXPLORE THE OPTIONS

Using the materials included in the Field Research section at the end of this book, conduct a thorough investigation of at least two career options for college graduates with a modern languages degree. You'll need a good selection of career books and resources and access to the Internet to complete this task. Here are some ways to put a degree in modern languages to work. Use this list for ideas but feel free to focus your exploration on another idea that interests you.

- College Professor
- Cruise Line Director
- Editor
- Foreign Correspondent
- Hotel Manager
- International Banker

- International Businessperson
- Interpreter
- Resort Manager
- Teacher (K–12)
- Tour Guide
- Translator

Field Research Worksheet

Now that you've learned a little about what a major in modern languages is like, think about what it means for you. Could this be a good choice? Can you say with reasonable certainty that it's not a good fit at all? Use the following planning worksheet to explain your response.

NO WAY!

Here are three reasons why I don't think this major would be a good choice for me.

_____

_____

_____

Stop! If you are sure this is not a major you want to pursue, don't waste another minute! Move on and explore another major.

A DEFINITE MAYBE

Here are three reasons why I think this major might be a good choice for me.

_____

_____

_____

Following are my plans to find out all I can about this major.

FIELD RESEARCH PROJECT 1: TALK ABOUT IT

I will use the materials included in the Field Research section of this book (Part 5) to conduct interviews with the following people:

_____ Senior completing a major in modern language

_____ Modern language professor

_____ Modern language professional

FIELD RESEARCH PROJECT 2: READ ABOUT IT

I will use the materials included in Part 5 of this book to review the following book(s) about potential career tracks:

_____

_____

FIELD RESEARCH PROJECT 3: EXPERIENCE IT

I have arranged a tour or job-shadowing experience at the following location and will use the materials included in Part 5 of this book to record my observations:

_____ Location

_____ Contact Person

_____ Date and Time of Appointment

FIELD RESEARCH PROJECT 4: EXPLORE THE OPTIONS

I want to find out all I can about the following career(s) and will use the materials included in Part 5 of this book to guide my investigation at the library and on the Internet:

_____ Career Choice #1

_____ Career Choice #2

_____

Student's Name and Date

_____ Field Research Plan Approved

_____ Field Research Plan Not Approved

Because:

_____

_____

_____

Instructor's Signature and Date

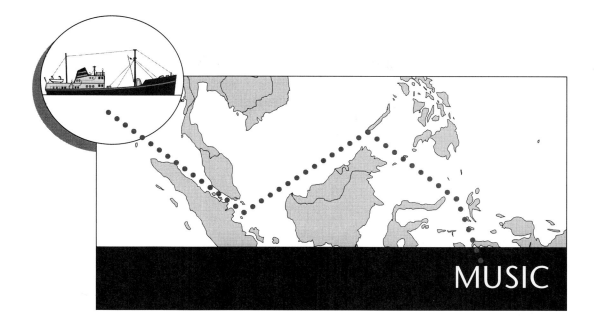

MUSIC

Is This Major for You?

- Are you musically inclined?
- Do you have an appreciation for all kinds of music?
- Have you been involved in the school band or orchestra?
- Have you succcessfully completed at least basic studies in the theory of music?
- Do you have a specific musical career path in mind?
- Have you ever written lyrics or music to a song?
- Have you ever performed in a musical production?

If you answer yes to several of these questions, keep reading to find out if a major in music is a good choice for you.

WHAT IS MUSIC?

As a liberal or fine arts discipline, music involves the systematic study, teaching, composition, and performance of folk, classical, and popular music. As a branch of commerce, the popular music industry centers on music for entertainment: its performance, production, publication, and distribution.

HISTORY AND BACKGROUND

There has been music as long as there have been human beings, for humans possess the most natural instrument of all, the voice. Music served early people as

Dr. Earl Henry, Music Professor at Webster University, contributed to this article.

part of social bonding, ritual, and communication. Songs about leaders, myths, and travel helped early communities record their important history.

Western music evolved from the early Christian church music, much of it in the form of free-flowing religious chants. In the 1300s, the Ars Nova in France and similar movements elsewhere in Europe brought structure to music using meter: that is, with regularly recurring strong and weak pulses. By 1600, Western music as we know it today had completed its basic evolution with the general acceptance of tonality (centering the listener's interest around one particular scale of tones of the major or minor mode). These intentional limitations allowed composers great flexibility in structuring compositions of considerable length and complexity. So strong was the influence of tonality, in fact, that although music changed considerably in style over the next 300 years (due in large part to technical improvements in instruments and the tastes of a rising middle-class society), the procedures and materials of composition employed during the Baroque, Classical, and Romantic eras (ca. 1600–1900) are virtually identical.

During the second half of the 19th century, a number of Western composers such as Chopin, Wagner, and Debussy, among others, became disenchanted with the basic tonal system and experimented with new sounds and combinations. In the early 20th century, Igor Stravinsky created successful musical works that largely abandoned traditional approaches to rhythm and meter; the Austrian composer Arnold Schoenberg devised serial composition, an entirely new and atonal system of music. While these and other truly innovative Western music have attracted interest among professionals, audiences for classical music (especially since 1945) have not only shrunk, but have consistently demanded "the classics." Widely accepted with audiences and consumers, on the other hand, American popular music, jazz, and rock (all rooted to some extent in the music of African slaves and their descendants), have rarely strayed from a highly colored, 18th century musical vocabulary and usage.

MUSIC TODAY

Throughout much of the world, the word "music" means Western pop music. Western composers continue to write music for art's sake, but their audience is limited. Accordingly, the future of music in the traditional European vein is unclear. With a generally apathetic listening public, the incentives for creating new music of serious artistic merit rest with the composers, their patrons, and educational and arts institutions. Most employment (and virtually all of the money) is available to commercial music ventures. Still, none of us knows what new developments in technology, perhaps just around the corner, will revolutionize our "use" of music as the phonograph, radio, and digital synthesizer have done in their respective eras in the 20th century.

WHAT COURSES DO YOU NEED TO TAKE?

There are a variety of paths to obtaining a degree in music. Depending upon the program in which you enroll, you can get a bachelor of arts in music, a bachelor of fine arts, a bachelor of music, a bachelor of arts in education, a bachelor of science, or a bachelor of music in music education. Regardless of the specific major area, the first two years of college study emphasize not only performance but also the composition and analysis of music throughout the range of Western literature. In addition, aural (sight singing and ear training) and keyboard skills are typically studied. Other courses include conducting, arranging, and ensemble work, and a concentration in the particular performance medium chosen. Requirements and electives are chosen from:

Composition and Arranging	History and Literature of Music
Contemporary Styles	Music Theory
Ear Training	

Courses regarding the business of music include:

Music Business	Music on Computer
Music Engineering	Music Management
Music Industry Financial Management	Music Production
	Music Technology

WHAT CAN YOU DO WITH A DEGREE IN MUSIC?

If you are thinking about centering your career on music, you might ask yourself an important question: "What does music mean to me?" If your concept of music revolves around rock and its stylistic derivatives, i.e. the "music of today," you might consider pursuing a degree in audio-visual production, media, business, or a related field, and supplementing these studies with music electives. If, on the other hand, you view music as a body of great works of art from many style periods, then the traditional music curriculum may be right for you. College music study will help you determine your natural talent, your potential, and your priorities.

Whether you are pop- or art-oriented, however, one fact is clear: the profession of music is highly competitive. Your performance, composition, analysis, or other work will be constantly compared with that of others. While there is employment each year for the very best musicians, many of those who major in music wind up earning a living in another field. Leaders in business and industry have long acknowledged that music students are good at many things. They deal, individually, with abstract concepts (tone quality, musical phrase, and line) and also with the challenges of a group effort (bands, choirs, and orchestras).

In the next ten to twenty years, musicians will continue to find work as ensemble performers, teachers, and, of course, employees of the music industry. The job outlook in public and private school music teaching (primary and secondary) is particularly favorable.

WHAT DO EXPERTS SAY ABOUT MUSIC?

Dr. Earl Henry, Music Professor at Webster University, offers this advice to prospective students:

What can a person expect during the course of study? Students can expect three to four hours per day of classes, two to three hours of practice, and one hour of musical ensemble. There will be several hours of study, a weekly lesson with an applied teacher, and concerts and performances throughout the year.

What are the characteristics of a successful student? A successful student is willing to spend the time and set priorities to determine her potential. This helps a person realize her level of commitment. Successful students are detail-oriented with work and practice. It helps to have a previous background in music.

What do you see for the future of the discipline? The future of the discipline is in flux, and that makes it exciting. Music majors, regardless of where they finally make a living, have an opportunity to influence the art of music. Will classical music die out, will a new form emerge? The key is versatility.

What makes the field exciting to you, personally, and why do you love what you do? This field is exciting to me as a teacher and theorist because I have the ability to convey the greatness of work we consider classical music. It's not going to disappear, as it's been around for centuries. I can explain it technically and in prose to those who may not have thought about it in these terms. Even though pop music vocabulary and thinking permeates people's perception of music, there is still the opportunity to help students think about the greatness of these works.

BEFORE YOU DECIDE . . .

Before you invest the next four years pursuing this field of study, invest a few hours in a thorough investigation of what a degree in music can do for you. Use the following suggestions and the worksheet at the end of this chapter to make a plan for conducting some field research. Once your plan is complete and approved by your instructor, proceed to Part 5, Field Research, where you'll find further instructions for making the most of these activities.

TALK ABOUT IT

Conduct interviews with the following three people (using the information included in the Field Research section in Part 5 of this book to guide your discussions):

- A senior completing a degree in music
- A music professor at your school
- A professional working in a music-related career

READ ABOUT IT

Following is a book listing that provides an overview of possible career options for someone with a degree in music.

- Field, Shelly. *Career Opportunities in the Music Industry*. New York: Facts on File, 1990.
- Goldberg, Jan. *Great Jobs for Music Majors*. Lincolnwood, IL: VGM Career Horizons, 1998.
- Riordan, James. *Making It in the New Music Business*. Cincinnati, OH: Writer's Digest Books, 1991.

- Siegel, Alan H. *Breaking Into the Music Business*. New York: Simon & Schuster, 1990.
- Uscher, Nancy. *Your Own Way in Music: A Career and Resource Guide*. New York: St. Martin's Press, 1990.
- Weissman, Dick. *The Music Business: Career Opportunities and Self-Defense*. New York: Crown Publishers, 1990.

EXPERIENCE IT

Seek out an opportunity to see what a degree in music can do for you in the workplace. Arrange a tour, a job-shadowing experience, or even a full-fledged internship at a place such as:

- A recording studio
- A concert promotion company
- An orchestra or opera production company
- A music publishing company
- A school band director's class
- A music retailer's store

Once you have scheduled a first appointment, use the information included in the Field Research section of this book to make the most of this experience.

EXPLORE THE OPTIONS

Using the materials included in the Field Research section at the end of this book, conduct a thorough investigation of at least two career options for college graduates with a music degree. You'll need a good selection of career books and resources and access to the Internet to complete this task. Here are some ways to put a degree in music to work. Use this list for ideas but feel free to focus your exploration on another idea that interests you.

- Agent
- Business Manager
- Choir Director
- Choreographer
- Composer
- Development Director
- Disc Jockey
- Entertainment Lawyer
- Events Coordinator
- Musician
- Music Librarian
- Music Therapist
- Music Video Producer
- Orchestra Director
- Publicist
- Publisher
- Retailer
- Singer
- Songwriter
- Sound Engineer
- Studio Producer

REFERENCE

Henry, Earl. *Sight Singing*. Upper Saddle River, NJ: Prentice Hall, 1997.

Now that you've learned a little about what a major in music is like, think about what it means for you. Could this be a good choice for you? Can you say with reasonable certainty that it's not a good fit at all? Use the following planning worksheet to explain your response.

NO WAY!

Here are three reasons why I don't think this major would be a good choice for me.

_____

_____

_____

Stop! If you are sure this is not a major you want to pursue, don't waste another minute! Move on and explore another major.

A DEFINITE MAYBE

Here are three reasons why I think this major might be a good choice for me.

_____

_____

_____

Following are my plans to find out all I can about this major.

FIELD RESEARCH PROJECT 1: TALK ABOUT IT

I will use the materials included in the Field Research section of this book (Part 5) to conduct interviews with the following people:

_____ Senior completing a major in music

_____ Music professor

_____ Music professional

FIELD RESEARCH PROJECT 2: READ ABOUT IT

I will use the materials included in Part 5 of this book to review the following book(s) about potential career tracks:

_____

_____

FIELD RESEARCH PROJECT 3: EXPERIENCE IT

I have arranged a tour or job-shadowing experience at the following location and will use the materials included in the Field Research section of this book to record my observations:

_____ Location

_____ Contact Person

_____ Date and Time of Appointment

FIELD RESEARCH PROJECT 4: EXPLORE THE OPTIONS

I want to find out all I can about the following career(s) and will use the materials included in Part 5 of this book to guide my investigation at the library and on the Internet:

_____ Career Choice #1

_____ Career Choice #2

· ·

_____

Student's Name and Date

_____ Field Research Plan Approved

_____ Field Research Plan Not Approved

Because:

_____

_____

_____

_____

Instructor's Signature and Date

· ·

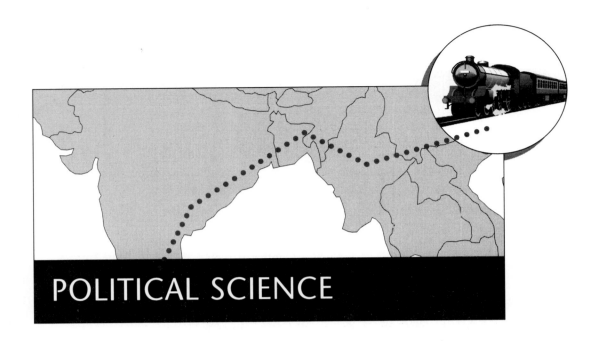

POLITICAL SCIENCE

Is This Major for You?

- Are you a politics junkie, always reading about some aspect of what's going on in the world of politics?
- Have you ever been actively involved in a political campaign?
- Have you ever run for a student governmental position?
- Did you particularly enjoy your high school civics, government, and world history classes?
- Are you able to listen to and respect other people's viewpoints?
- Do you have the ability to look at both sides of an issue and formulate your own opinion based on fact and reason?
- Are you interested in the role various forms of government plays in world affairs?

If you answered yes to several of these questions, keep reading to find out if a major in political science is a good choice for you.

INTRODUCTION

Politics is the activity by which people "try to get more of whatever there is to get—money, prestige, jobs, respect, sex, and even power itself." Politics occurs in many different settings: the office, where an account executive successfully angles for a promotion by knowing the right people; the school, where a mediocre student takes advantage of an offer to raise his grade by doing extra work for the teacher; and labor organizations, where promising to support a new policy at a

Dr. Thomas Dye, Political Science Professor at Florida State University, contributed to this article.

factory earns a large group of workers better benefits. Any time individuals or organizations maneuver themselves to obtain advantage over others, politics is at work. Political science limits its perspective to politics in government.

WHAT IS POLITICAL SCIENCE?

Political science is the study of who gets what, when, and how. The *who* are the participants, from voters to bureaucrats. The *what* are public policies—governmental decisions concerning the thousands of political issues it reviews. The *when* and *how* are the political processes, from campaigns and elections to the decisions of the president and higher courts. The governmental politics of political science are distinguished from the politics of the rest of society because governmental decisions extend to the whole society. Only the government can legitimately use force; people accept the necessity for the government to act forcefully.

HISTORY AND BACKGROUND

Aristotle, the Greek philosopher, called political science the "master science" because he felt that all other sciences depended upon it: history, law, philosophy, and sociology, among others, provide a framework for political perspective. Aristotle believed that the purpose of political science was to provide a model for political order—to establish maximum justice while maintaining stability. This simple idea is as applicable today as it was in his time. Consider nuclear war. If the fruits of scientific knowledge cannot be managed peacefully, the results could be disastrous for humankind.

A medieval movement called "scholasticism" placed the Greek ideas of political science within the framework of Christianity and emphasized rights and responsibilities of the individual with respect to the processes of government. These theories were challenged in the early 1600s by secularism, which favored what was believed to be a realistic view of politics, separate from religion. In 1689, English philosopher John Locke published *Two Treatises of Government*, which championed a new perspective called "constitutionalism." It called for a separation of governing powers and emphasized basic human rights. Locke's writings became the basis of the United States Constitution. Other ideas about organizing political governments have appeared as liberalism, socialism, communism, and democracy.

POLITICAL SCIENCE TODAY

Political scientists today are concerned with practical improvement in society and political reform. They increasingly use descriptive, analytical, and quantitative studies to achieve political progress. As we move toward a global community, these studies include every nation in the world. There are six main fields in political science in the United States today:

POLITICAL THEORY AND PHILOSOPHY. Study of the history of political thought as the basis for exploring and understanding empirical politics (politics based on experience). This area examines the different approaches to government and how power is gained or lost.

COMPARATIVE GOVERNMENT. Studies that compare political practices and philosophies of two or more countries.

AMERICAN GOVERNMENT AND POLITICS. Study of the national, state, and local governments of the United States.

PUBLIC ADMINISTRATION. Deals with modern governmental administrative activities.

INTERNATIONAL RELATIONS. One of the most important areas of study today; deals with international law and diplomacy, as well as defense policies.

POLITICAL BEHAVIOR. Using perspectives of behavioral sciences, such as anthropology and sociology, studies the ways in which people respond to political circumstances and influences.

WHAT COURSES DO YOU NEED TO TAKE?

Political science majors are often combined with minors in supporting disciplines, depending upon area of interest and career direction. In addition to a school's core requirements and major requirements, courses in analytical skills, writing and speaking, and computer technology are important. Courses for major emphasis include:

American Political System	Microeconomics
Early Political Thought	Modern Political Thought
Introduction to Political Science	Principles of Economics
Law, Politics, and Justice	Research Methods
Macroeconomics	Western Civilization/U.S. History

WHAT CAN YOU DO WITH A DEGREE IN POLITICAL SCIENCE?

Political science graduates find careers in law, government, urban planning, and journalism. There are public service jobs in any branch or agency of the federal, state, and local governments. There are positions in the federal government as interns with Congress, foreign and domestic teachers, intelligence personnel, inspectors, and Congressional staff members. State and local governments offer positions on staffs of executive departments and agencies that deal with zoning, public and highway safety, welfare, traffic control and transportation, resource management, and industrial development.

Private interest groups employ political science graduates as lobbyists to represent their interests. International organizations and businesses employ graduates to serve as liaisons between private and public interests. Graduates find work within political campaigns, and those with excellent writing skills enter journalism as political reporters.

Advanced degrees offer the opportunity to teach at the university level, participate in research projects, and work for Congressional committees as staff and research members.

WHAT DO EXPERTS SAY ABOUT POLITICAL SCIENCE?

Dr. Thomas Dye, Political Science Professor at Florida State University, offers this advice to prospective students:

What can a person expect during the course of study? Students will learn how to realistically appraise prospects for government and public policy. They will learn how to evaluate what politics means in their lives and learn what possibilities exist.

What are the characteristics of a successful student? Beyond anything else, successful students have the ability to understand, if not agree with, other people's points of view.

What do you see for the future of the discipline? Political science will continue to be a central part of a liberal arts education and in demand as globalization continues.

What makes this field exciting to you, personally, and why do you love what you do? Politics is very fascinating to me because it's a struggle for power. It's never-ending, always interesting, and occasionally entertaining!

BEFORE YOU DECIDE . . .

Before you invest the next four years pursuing this field of study, invest a few hours in a thorough investigation of what a degree in political science can do for you. Use the following suggestions and the worksheet at the end of this chapter to make a plan for conducting some field research. Once your plan is complete and approved by your instructor, proceed to Part 5, Field Research, where you'll find further instructions for making the most of these activities.

TALK ABOUT IT

Conduct interviews with the following three people (using the information included in the Field Research section in Part 5 of this book to guide your discussions):

- A senior completing a degree in political science
- A political science professor at your school
- A professional working in a political science-related career

READ ABOUT IT

Following is a book listing that provides an overview of possible career options for someone with a degree in political science.

- Baxter, Neale. *Opportunities in Federal Government Careers*. Lincolnwood, IL: VGM Career Horizons, 1994.
- Career Associates. *Career Choices for Students of Political Science and Government*. New York: Walker, 1990.
- Carland, Maria Pinto. *Careers in International Affairs*. Washington, D.C.: Georgetown University Press, 1996.
- Hibbing, John R. *Congressional Careers: Contours of Life in the U.S. House of Representatives*. Chapel Hill, NC: University of North Carolina Press, 1991.
- Jebens, Harley. *100 Jobs in Social Change*. New York: Macmillan, 1997.
- Pitz, Mary Elizabeth. *Careers in Government*. Lincolnwood, IL: VGM Career Horizons, 1995.
- Powers, Linda. *Careers in International Affairs*. Washington, D.C.: Georgetown University School of Foreign Service, 1991.
- Rajala, Hope M. and Neale J. Baxter. *Opportunities in State and Local Government Careers*. Lincolnwood, IL: VGM Career Horizons, 1992.

EXPERIENCE IT

Seek out an opportunity to see what a degree in political science can do for you in the workplace. Arrange a tour, a job-shadowing experience, or even a full-fledged internship at a place such as:

- A municipal center of government
- The office of a state legislator or government official
- The office of a national legislator
- A law firm
- The legal affairs department of a corporation
- The chambers of a judge
- Headquarters of a think tank, public affairs agency, or special interest group
- Headquarters for a political party

Once you have scheduled a first appointment, use the information included in the Field Research section of this book to make the most of this experience.

EXPLORE THE OPTIONS

Using the materials included in the Field Research section at the end of this book, conduct a thorough investigation of at least two career options for college graduates with a political science degree. You'll need a good selection of career books and resources and access to the Internet to complete this task. Here are some ways to put a degree in political science to work. Use this list for ideas but feel free to focus your exploration on another idea that interests you.

- Association Executive
- Attorney
- Banker
- Business Administrator
- College Professor
- Congressional Staffperson
- Diplomat
- Editor

- Foreign Service Officer
- Governmental Official
- Governmental Relations Manager
- Intelligence Officer
- Investor Relations Manager
- Journalist
- Legislative Affairs Director
- Liaison
- Lobbyist
- Military Officer
- Policy Analyst
- Political Scientist
- Politician
- Public Administrator
- Regional Planner
- Think Tank Fellow
- Urban Planner

REFERENCE

Dye, Thomas R. *Politics in America*. Upper Saddle River, NJ: Prentice Hall, 1997.

Now that you've learned a little about what a major in political science is like, think about what it means for you. Could this be a good choice for you? Can you say with reasonable certainty that it's not a good fit at all? Use the following planning worksheet to explain your response.

NO WAY!

Here are three reasons why I don't think this major would be a good choice for me.

_____

_____

_____

Stop! If you are sure this is not a major you want to pursue, don't waste another minute! Move on and explore another major.

A DEFINITE MAYBE

Here are three reasons why I think this major might be a good choice for me.

_____

_____

_____

Following are my plans to find out all I can about this major.

FIELD RESEARCH PROJECT 1: TALK ABOUT IT

I will use the materials included in the Field Research section of this book (Part 5) to conduct interviews with the following people:

_____ Senior completing a major in political science

_____ Political science professor

_____ Political science professional

FIELD RESEARCH PROJECT 2: READ ABOUT IT

I will use the materials included in Part 5 of this book to review the following book(s) about potential career tracks:

_____

_____

Field Research Worksheet

FIELD RESEARCH PROJECT 3: EXPERIENCE IT

I have arranged a tour or job-shadowing experience at the following location and will use the materials included in Part 5 of this book to record my observations:

_____ Location

_____ Contact Person

_____ Date and Time of Appointment

FIELD RESEARCH PROJECT 4: EXPLORE THE OPTIONS

I want to find out all I can about the following career(s) and will use the materials included in Part 5 of this book to guide my investigation at the library and on the Internet:

_____ Career Choice #1

_____ Career Choice #2

· ·

_____

Student's Name and Date

_____ Field Research Plan Approved
_____ Field Research Plan Not Approved

Because:

_____

_____

_____

Instructor's Signature and Date

· ·

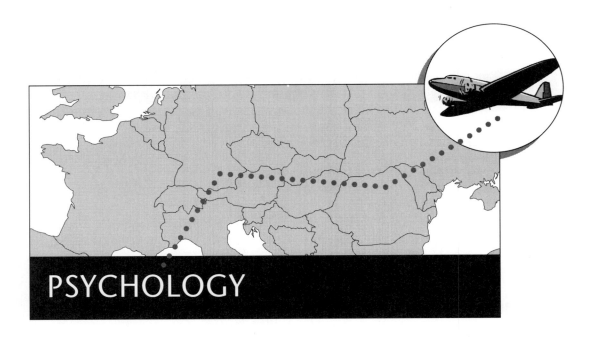

PSYCHOLOGY

Is This Major for You?

- Are you a good listener?
- Do you have a genuine interest in helping people?
- Are you trustworthy and able to keep secrets?
- Do you enjoy reading and learning new techniques?
- Are you comfortable dealing with people in a variety of situations?
- Would you consider it an honor to help people sort through personal problems no matter how trivial or traumatic?
- Does the idea of becoming a "mind investigator" appeal to you?
- Would you be interested in a career with a health or educational facility (where approximately 70% of psychologists are employed)?

If you answered yes to several of these questions, keep reading to find out if a major in psychology is a good choice for you.

INTRODUCTION

Have you ever been curious about why people behave as they do? Why, at the scene of the same car accident, does one person cry, one person go for help, and one person rush toward the smoking vehicle to rescue the victims? What makes people tick? How do their behaviors affect their lives? If finding the answers to these questions is an exciting prospect, psychology may be the major for you!

Dr. Stephen Davis, Psychology Professor at Emporia State University, contributed to this article.

WHAT IS PSYCHOLOGY?

Psychology is the science that studies why human beings and animals behave as they do. It involves looking at behavioral patterns and processes from a biological and physiological point of view. From these perspectives, psychology is the study of perceptions, motivations, learning, memory, attitudes, and emotions. Psychologists study these areas through scientific observation, case histories, and surveys. The results of their research lead to methods that help people improve personal and interpersonal behavior and discover new skills and directions in their lives.

HISTORY AND BACKGROUND

The word *psychology* comes from the Greek *psyche* (mind or soul) and *logos* (the study of). Early Greek philosophers were the first to organize thoughts about human behavior. Psychology was considered a philosophical subject until the late 1800s, when German philosopher Wilhelm Wundt began the first scientific inquiries into psychological behavior. From this emerged the schools of thought that form the basis of today's discipline.

PSYCHOLOGY TODAY

Psychologists today are interested in a diversity of topics. They do not necessarily align themselves strictly with any one approach, choosing instead to use the approach most appropriate to each issue they encounter. This is called an "eclectic approach" to psychology. A growing number of psychologists do little or no research, preferring instead to work directly with people as health service providers. Clinical psychologists specialize in helping people with behavioral or emotional problems caused by adjusting to the demands of life. Clinical psychologists should not be confused with psychiatrists, who are medical doctors trained to assess behavioral problems from a medical perspective. Another specialty similar to clinical psychology is counseling psychology. Counseling psychologists work with less serious problems than do clinical psychologists, issues like vocational decisions or physical handicaps. As the pressures of entering the new millennium affect all areas of personal, corporate, and educational life, psychology becomes an important tool that affects every aspect of modern life.

WHAT COURSES DO YOU NEED TO TAKE?

A bachelor of arts in psychology includes the basic psych requirements with a minor in the arts or sciences, other than biology, chemistry, computer science, math, or physics. A bachelor of science includes the basic psych requirements with a minor in biology, chemistry, computer science, math, or physics. Most specialized areas that include diagnosis and counseling of any kind require postgraduate work, but many majors in specific areas of concentration are achieved with carefully designed undergraduate degree plans. The following is a list of requirements and electives for an undergraduate major in psychology:

History of Psychology

Introduction to Psychology

Introduction to Statistics

Research Methods—Theory and Application

Electives can be chosen from among:

Abnormal Psychology

Adolescent Psychology

Adult Psychology

Animal Behavior

Child Psychology

Human Cognition

Neuroscience

Personality Theory

Psychology of Perception

Social Psychology

WHAT CAN YOU DO WITH A DEGREE IN PSYCHOLOGY?

Many people believe that the only job of a psychologist is to provide diagnostic and therapeutic services to people with mental disorders. There are many other specialties beyond clinical and counseling psychology. Psychology deals with human behavior and its motivations. A growing number of industries are addressing the mental and emotional needs of their employees and consumers as important for harmony and productivity. Following are a few examples of the directions one can take with an undergraduate degree:

With a business minor:

Advertising Trainee/Agent

Customer Relations

Employment Counselor

Insurance Agent

Loan Officer

Marketing Researcher/Representative

Personnel Administrator

Public Relations

Sales Manager

With a minor in family and child studies, health-related studies, or sociology:

Affirmative Action Officer

Behavioral Analyst

Community Services Worker

Counselor Aide

Day Care Supervisor (children or adults)

Rehab Advisor

Social Services Director

Volunteer Services Director

The majority of psychology majors want to enter the area of counseling and research, which requires an advanced degree. In addition to an advanced degree, some positions require that you be licensed by the state in which you work. The American Psychological Association publishes a pamphlet that will give you more information about careers and licensing requirements. The following are some of the specialized professions for psychologists:

COUNSELING PSYCHOLOGY. Helps people deal with normal problems of adjustment to changes in their lives. Counseling psychologists work for clinics, agencies, or directly with individuals through private practice.

ENVIRONMENTAL PSYCHOLOGY. Concerned with design of physical environments to enhance successful living and making physical settings functional and comfortable for individuals and groups. Environmental psychologists work with architects, urban planners, and in natural environments with biologists and conservationists.

HEALTH PSYCHOLOGY. Deals with health education and diagnosis, treatment and prevention of illness. Health psychologists help people change their attitudes about risk-related behaviors, such as smoking and obesity, that are associated with poor health.

EDUCATIONAL PSYCHOLOGY. Seeks to increase knowledge about teaching/learning processes and to apply this knowledge to school and work settings through improving instruction and curriculum. Educational psychologists work directly with students and businesses that provide education for career enhancement.

MEDIA PSYCHOLOGY. Focuses on understanding how electronic and printed information and formats affect individuals, especially children who are influenced by exposure to today's television and on-line media. Media psychologists are employed in journalism, broadcasting, and education where they assist media personnel in developing positive formats.

LEGAL PSYCHOLOGY. Applies psychology to improving laws and helping individuals understand the legal system. Legal psychologists consult with educational groups and work with juries in the courts.

ABNORMAL PSYCHOLOGY. The application of psychological science to the study of mental disorders. Professions in abnormal psychology are related to the medical field and require intense postgraduate specialization.

CLINICAL PSYCHOLOGY. Clinical psychologists diagnose and treat mental disorders of all kinds, provide counseling services, conduct research, and teach. This requires five years of graduate study and a one-year internship to earn a doctorate.

PSYCHIATRY. Psychiatrists are physicians who specialize in diagnosis and treatment of mental dysfunctions. This requires a four-year specialization, focusing on abnormal behavior, following the completion of medical school and internship.

SOCIAL WORK. Social workers place more emphasis on the social and cultural aspects of behavior. Psychiatric social workers treat mental health problems through schools, hospitals, social services agencies, courts and prisons; their work often includes dealing with cross-cultural behavior.

WHAT DO EXPERTS SAY ABOUT PSYCHOLOGY?

Dr. Stephen Davis, Psychology Professor at Emporia State University, offers this advice to prospective students:

What can a person expect during the course of study? Students can expect to be intellectually challenged with new ideas, concepts, and research findings during their program of study in the science of psychology. These new ideas, concepts, and research findings cover the full range of human experience from basic biological processes to social interactions.

What are the characteristics of a successful student? The successful psychology student has strong internal motivation, good study habits, and the ability to accept and appreciate differences in people and cultures.

What do you see for the future of this discipline? The future for psychology is bright and will continue to be so well into the next century. Why? Psychology is one of the fastest growing majors in college. Moreover, the demands for counseling and clinical psychologists, neuropsychologists, industrial-organizational psychologists, school and educational psychologists, forensic psychologists, and other psychological specialties have grown at an unprecedented rate.

The biggest challenges facing psychology are those created by technology and prosperity. As technology advances, it is important for psychologists to remain current in their knowledge of new techniques, equipment, and procedures. As psychology continues to grow and prosper, it has become a highly specialized and diversified field with numerous subareas and specialties. It is a challenge for psychologists to know and appreciate the breadth and depth of the field.

What makes this field exciting to you, personally, and why do you love what you do? The endless array of human behavior and the mysteries to be solved concerning this behavior make psychology a fascinating field that holds my interest as no other. My interest in human and animal behavior initially prompted me to choose psychology as a career.

BEFORE YOU DECIDE . . .

Before you invest the next four years pursuing this field of study, invest a few hours in a thorough investigation of what a degree in psychology can do for you. Use the following suggestions and the worksheet at the end of this chapter to make a plan for conducting some field research. Once your plan is complete and approved by your instructor, proceed to Part 5, Field Research, where you'll find further instructions for making the most of these activities.

TALK ABOUT IT

Conduct interviews with the following three people (using the information included in the Field Research section at the back of this book to guide your discussions):

- A senior completing a degree in psychology
- A psychology professor at your school
- A professional working in a psychology-related career

READ ABOUT IT

Following is a book listing that provides an overview of possible career options for someone with a degree in psychology.

- Baxter, Neale. *Opportunities in Counseling and Development Careers*. Lincolnwood, IL: NTC Publishing, 1994.
- Collison, Brooke B. and Nancy J. Garfield. *Careers in Counseling and Human Service*. Bristol, PA: Taylor and Francis, 1996.
- DeGalan, Julie and Stephen Lambert. *Great Jobs for Psychology Majors*. Lincolnwood, IL: VGM Career Horizons, 1995.
- Schmidt, Peggy. *Career Choices for the 90's: Psychology*. New York: Walker, 1990.
- Schmolling, Paul. *Careers in Mental Health: A Guide to Helping Others*. Garrett Park, MD: Garrett Park Press, 1986.

- Steinberg, Robert J. *Career Paths in Psychology*. Washington, D.C.: American Psychology Association, 1997.
- Super, Charles. *Opportunities in Psychology Careers*. Lincolnwood, IL: NTC Publishing, 1994.

EXPERIENCE IT

Seek out an opportunity to see what a degree in psychology can do for you in the workplace. Arrange a tour, a job-shadowing experience, or even a full-fledged internship at a place such as:

- A drug rehabilitation clinic
- A psychological testing center
- A psychological practice
- A county social services department
- A nonprofit agency focused on solving a sound issue you have an interest in
- A corporate human resources department
- A mental health hospital

Once you have scheduled a first appointment, use the information included in the Field Research section of this book to make the most of this experience.

EXPLORE THE OPTIONS

Using the materials included in the Field Research section at the end of this book, conduct a thorough investigation of at least two career options for college graduates with a psychology degree. You'll need a good selection of career books and resources and access to the Internet to complete this task.

Here are some ways to put a degree in psychology to work. Use this list for ideas but feel free to focus your exploration on another idea that interests you.

- Affirmative Action Officer
- Behavioral Analyst
- Career Counselor
- Corporate Counselor
- Corporate Trainer
- Direct Marketer
- Employee Benefits Administrator
- Employment Counselor
- Health Services Administrator
- Human Resources Administrator
- Insurance Agent
- Lawyer
- Marketing Specialist
- Nonprofit Agency Director
- Psychiatrist
- Psychologist
- Researcher
- Salesperson
- School Counselor
- Social Services Administrator
- Social Worker
- Teacher
- Volunteer Services Administrator

REFERENCE

Davis, Stephen and Joseph Palladino. *Psychology 2*. Upper Saddle River, NJ: Prentice Hall, 1997.

Now that you've learned a little about what a major in psychology is like, think about what it means for you. Could this be a good choice for you? Can you say with reasonable certainty that it's not a good fit at all? Use the following planning worksheet to explain your response.

NO WAY!

Here are three reasons why I don't think this major would be a good choice for me.

_____

_____

_____

Stop! If you are sure this is not a major you want to pursue, don't waste another minute! Move on and explore another major.

A DEFINITE MAYBE

Here are three reasons why I think this major might be a good choice for me.

_____

_____

_____

Following are my plans to find out all I can about this major.

FIELD RESEARCH PROJECT 1: TALK ABOUT IT

I will use the materials included in the Field Research section of this book (Part 5) to conduct interviews with the following people:

_____ Senior completing a major in psychology

_____ Psychology professor

_____ Psychology professional

FIELD RESEARCH PROJECT 2: READ ABOUT IT

I will use the materials included in Part 5 of this book to review the following book(s) about potential career tracks:

_____

_____

Field Research Worksheet

FIELD RESEARCH PROJECT 3: EXPERIENCE IT

I have arranged a tour or job-shadowing experience at the following location and will use the materials included in Part 5 of this book to record my observations:

_____ Location

_____ Contact Person

_____ Date and Time of Appointment

FIELD RESEARCH PROJECT 4: EXPLORE THE OPTIONS

I want to find out all I can about the following career(s) and will use the materials included in Part 5 of this book to guide my investigation at the library and on the Internet:

_____ Career Choice #1

_____ Career Choice #2

. . . .

_____

Student's Name and Date

_____ Field Research Plan Approved

_____ Field Research Plan Not Approved

Because:

_____

_____

_____

Instructor's Signature and Date

. . . .

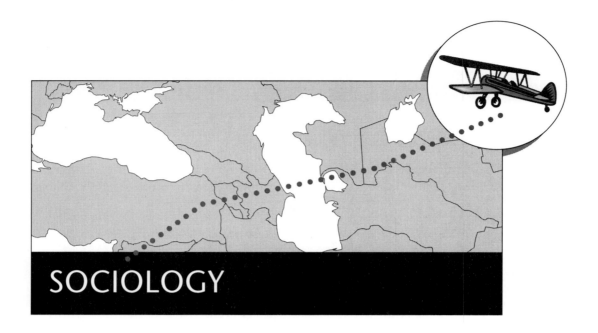

SOCIOLOGY

Is This Major for You?

- Are you curious about why things are as they are?
- Do you want to make the world a better place?
- Are you a people watcher—always interested in what others are doing, what they are wearing, and how they react to various situations?
- Can people generally count on you to lend a hand when they need help?
- Are you willing to tackle some tough issues in your work and ready to accept answers from unexpected places?
- Have you ever worked as a volunteer for an organization with a mission of helping others in need?
- Are you fascinated by the customs and cultures of other peoples?

If you answered yes to several of these questions, keep reading to find out if a major in sociology is a good choice for you.

INTRODUCTION

The 5.7 billion people on Earth today are members of a single biological species: homo sapiens. Even so, there are a multitude of differences among peoples of the world. Some are lifestyle differences and matters of convention—the Chinese wear white at funerals while people in the United States prefer black. In China, the number four is associated with bad luck; in the U. S., thirteen is considered unlucky. At weddings, U. S. couples kiss, Koreans bow, and a Cambodian groom touches his nose to the bride's cheek. The world over, people

Dr. John Macionis, Sociology Professor at Kenyon College, contributed to this article.

wear much or little clothing, have many or few children, venerate or shunt the elderly, are peaceful or warlike, embrace different religious beliefs, and enjoy different kinds of art and music. Although we are the same creatures biologically, we are strikingly different in our tastes, behaviors, and beliefs. This capacity for startling difference is a wonder of our species: the expression of human culture. The study of this expression is sociology.

WHAT IS SOCIOLOGY?

Sociology is the systematic study of how human societies shape the lives of the people who live in them. Individuals make many important decisions in the course of a day, and these are not made by sheer chance. The decisions are made within the context of society—a family, a school, a nation, an entire world. The essential wisdom of sociology is that the social world guides our actions and life choices just as the seasons influence our choice of activities and clothing. Because sociologists know a great deal about how society works, they can predict how we will behave.

HISTORY AND BACKGROUND

From the time of the ancient Greek philosophers until the early 1800s, many great thinkers studied the nature of society. They looked at society in the context of ideals, of what it should do, and they constructed images of the perfect society. In 1838, French philosopher August Comte introduced the *sociological* point of view, or looking at society for what it is and trying to understand how it operates.

Comte envisioned sociology as the scientific study of what society is rather than what it ought to be. He developed the theory of positivism, which stated that social behavior and events could be observed and measured scientifically. He looked at agrarian/industrial economies, political change, and urban growth as significant historical factors that influence change in society. Today, sociologists look at social questions in the context of three major theoretical paradigms that allow them to effectively analyze virtually any dimension of society.

SOCIOLOGY TODAY

Sociologists today study specific groups and types of people within a society rather than draw conclusions about overall social conditions. The changes in these conditions and lifestyles in general have been dramatic since the social upheavals of the 1960s and have been the subjects of many sociological inquiries. The use of computers and more reliable surveying techniques has improved the field.

Social psychology is an important application of sociology today. Social psychologists study the social influence that individuals have on one another and within groups, and the influence of groups on one another. Issues such as conformity, leadership, prejudice, morale, attitude, and child-rearing are examined by social psychologists. Results of studies are used to understand problems of intergroup tensions and prejudices, industrial morale, and international relations, increasingly important issues as our society enters an age of globalization.

WHAT COURSES DO YOU NEED TO TAKE?

Following are the types of courses typically associated with a degree in sociology:

Contemporary Social Theory	Research Methods
History of Social Theory	Statistics
Introduction to Sociology	Urban Sociology

WHAT CAN YOU DO WITH A DEGREE IN SOCIOLOGY?

Sociological study is wide-ranging, from crime, social inequality, aging, family life, and urban living to how new information technology is changing our lives. Sociologists go into careers in criminal justice, social work, gerontology (the study of aging), and demography (the study of population changes), as well as business, medicine, and law.

A bachelor's degree is a good start for a career in business or law enforcement. Careers in business include government administration, biographer, consumer services, personnel and placement manager, public services educator, probation officer, statistician, urban planning, and technical writer. A master's degree and a doctorate open the door to teaching or research and are needed to obtain positions in any area of clinical social work.

WHAT DO EXPERTS SAY ABOUT SOCIOLOGY?

Dr. John Macionis, Sociology Professor at Kenyon College, offers this advice to prospective students:

What can a person expect during the course of study? Most people who take an introductory course are excited by how different the world seems when viewed sociologically. There is much to learn, of course, and majors may well encounter challenging courses in theory and statistical research.

What are the characteristics of a successful student? Successful sociologists are curious people. They are individuals who want to know why things are the way they are. Often, they are people who would like to change society in some way.

What do you see for the future of the discipline? There will always be a demand for sociological skills. The rapid social change taking place in the United States, as well as in other parts of the world, stimulate demand for men and women with sociological training.

What are the challenges facing this field? Challenges facing sociology today include connecting the field's knowledge to the kinds of jobs majors are seeking. To some degree, sociologists have assumed that the "purest" work involves abstract critique of society; the field would benefit from a renewed focus on the career goals of students.

What makes this field exciting to you, personally, and why do you love what you do? I am passionate about sociology because it is fun to do. It opens your mind and provides many answers where you never even knew there were questions!

BEFORE YOU DECIDE . . .

Before you invest the next four years pursuing this field of study, invest a few hours in a thorough investigation of what a degree in sociology can do for you. Use the following suggestions and the worksheet at the end of this chapter to make a plan for conducting some field research. Once your plan is complete and approved by your instructor, proceed to Part 5, Field Research, where you'll find further instructions for making the most of these activities.

TALK ABOUT IT

Conduct interviews with the following three people (using the information included in the Field Research section in Part 5 of this book to guide your discussions):

- A senior completing a degree in sociology
- A sociology professor at your school
- A professional working in a sociology-related career

READ ABOUT IT

Following is a book listing that provides an overview of possible career options for someone with a degree in sociology.

- Colvin, Donna. *Good Works: A Guide to Careers in Social Change*. New York: Barricade Books, 1994.
- Eberts, Marjorie and Margaret Gisler. *Careers for Good Samaritans*. Lincolnwood, IL: VGM Career Horizons, 1991.
- Everett, Melissa. *Making a Living While Making a Difference: A Guide to Creating Careers with Conscience*. New York: Bantam Books, 1993.
- Garner, Geraldine O. *Careers in Social and Rehabilitation Services*. Lincolnwood, IL: VGM Career Horizons, 1994.
- Ginsberg, Leon H. *Careers in Social Work*. Needham Heights, MA: Allyn & Bacon, 1998.
- Grobman, Linda M. *Days in the Lives of Social Workers: 41 Professionals Tell Real Life Stories from Social Work Practice*. Harrisburg, PA: White Hat Communications, 1996.
- Jebens, Harley. *100 Jobs in Social Change*. New York: Macmillan, 1996.
- Marik, Roseanne. *Opportunities in Social Science Careers*. Lincolnwood, IL: NTC Publishing, 1990.
- McAdam, Terry. *Careers in the Nonprofit Sector*. Detroit: The Taft Group, 1986.
- Morgan, Bradley J. *Mental Health and Social Work Career Directory*. Detroit: Visible Ink Press, 1993.
- Stephens, W. Richard. *Careers in Sociology*. Needham Heights, MA: Allyn & Bacon, 1994.

EXPERIENCE IT

Seek out an opportunity to see what a degree in sociology can do for you in the workplace. Arrange a tour, a job-shadowing experience, or even a full-fledged internship at a place such as:

- A criminal detention center
- A social services agency
- The human services department of a corporation
- A mental health facility
- A market research firm

Once you have scheduled a first appointment, use the information included in the Field Research section of this book to make the most of this experience.

EXPLORE THE OPTIONS

Using the materials included in the Field Research section at the end of this book, conduct a thorough investigation of at least two career options for college graduates with a sociology degree. You'll need a good selection of career books and resources and access to the Internet to complete this task. Here are some ways to put a degree in sociology to work. Use this list for ideas but feel free to focus your exploration on another idea that interests you.

- Biographer
- Business Administrator
- College Professor
- Consumer Services Manager
- Corporate Trainer
- Demographer
- Detective
- Health Services Administrator
- Investigator
- Law Enforcement Officer
- Nonprofit Agency Director

- Personnel Manager
- Probation Officer
- Public Service Educator
- Researcher
- Salesperson
- School Administrator
- Social Psychologist
- Social Worker
- Statistician
- Technical Writer
- Urban Planner

REFERENCE

Macionis, John J. *Sociology*. Upper Saddle River, NJ: Prentice Hall, 1997.

Field Research Worksheet

Now that you've learned a little about what a major in sociology is like, think about what it means for you. Could this be a good choice? Can you say with reasonable certainty that it's not a good fit at all? Use the following planning worksheet to explain your response.

NO WAY!

Here are three reasons why I don't think this major would be a good choice for me.

_____

_____

_____

Stop! If you are sure this is not a major you want to pursue, don't waste another minute! Move on and explore another major.

A DEFINITE MAYBE

Here are three reasons why I think this major might be a good choice for me.

_____

_____

_____

Following are my plans to find out all I can about this major.

FIELD RESEARCH PROJECT 1: TALK ABOUT IT

I will use the materials included in the Field Research section of this book (Part 5) to conduct interviews with the following people:

_____ Senior completing a major in sociology

_____ Sociology professor

_____ Sociology professional

FIELD RESEARCH PROJECT 2 READ ABOUT IT

I will use the materials included in Part 5 of this book to review the following book(s) about potential career tracks:

_____

_____

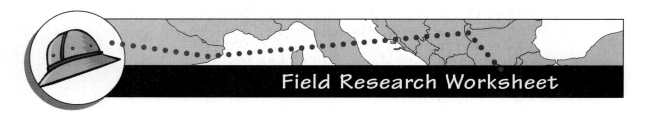

FIELD RESEARCH PROJECT 3: EXPERIENCE IT

I have arranged a tour or job-shadowing experience at the following location and will use the materials included in Part 5 of this book to record my observations:

_____ Location

_____ Contact Person

_____ Date and Time of Appointment

FIELD RESEARCH PROJECT 4: EXPLORE THE OPTIONS

I want to find out all I can about the following career(s) and will use the materials included in Part 5 of this book to guide my investigation at the library and on the Internet:

_____ Career Choice #1

_____ Career Choice #2

_____

Student's Name and Date

_____ Field Research Plan Approved

_____ Field Research Plan Not Approved

Because:

_____

_____

_____

Instructor's Signature and Date

3 Business

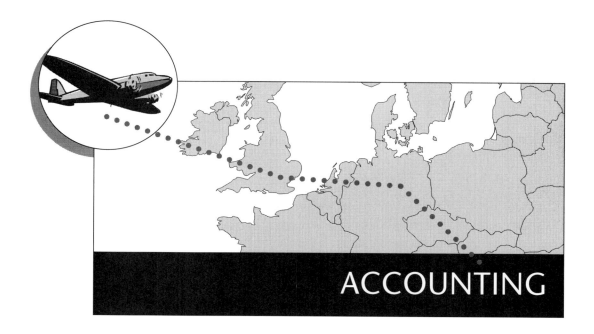

ACCOUNTING

Is This Major for You?

- Do you enjoy math and are you good at working numbers?
- Are you detail oriented—precise to the penny, so to speak?
- Does the idea of a number-intensive career appeal to you?
- Can other people trust you with their money?
- Can you balance a checkbook, and do you have a good sense of your personal expenses?
- Can you keep track of lots of details and stay on top of several simultaneous projects?
- Do you enjoy business math and accounting courses? (This is one major where the classes you'll take are very similar to the type of work you'll actually do on the job. So, if you don't like the classes, you won't like the work.)

If you answered yes to several of these questions, keep reading and find out if an accounting major is a good choice for you.

INTRODUCTION

How much do you spend every month? You may pay rent or buy food, gas, clothing, and other necessities. And, of course, there's the weekend money you want to spend. How do you make sure that you'll have enough money to cover all of this? If you know where your money is going and you make decisions on how to spend it, you're already using a basic accounting system. If you think you might like to do this on a larger scale for a business, then the field of accounting may be for you! And, by the way, lest you fear that this career may not be exciting

Dr. Charles Horngren, Accounting Professor at Stanford University, contributed to this article.

enough for you, keep in mind that it was FBI accountants who brought down the notorious mobster Al Capone!

WHAT IS ACCOUNTING?

Accounting is the system that measures business activities, processes that information into reports, and communicates the results to decision-makers. For this reason it is called "the language of business." What grammar is to English composition, accounting is to business. There is much more to accounting than bookkeeping. Bookkeeping is the procedural element (much as arithmetic is a procedural element of mathematics). Accounting is much more than procedures—it is a process that begins and ends with decision-making. Accounting is an important function of a successful business because it provides vital information that enables managers in production, marketing, and personnel to make informed decisions.

HISTORY AND BACKGROUND

Some scholars claim that writing arose in order to record accounting information. Indeed, accounting records date back to the ancient civilizations of China, Babylonia, Greece, and Egypt. The rulers of these civilizations used accounting to keep track of the costs of labor and materials used in building structures such as the great pyramids. The need for accounting has existed as long as there has been business activity.

In the 19th century, the growth of corporations spurred the development of accounting. Corporation owners (stockholders) were no longer the managers of their businesses but still needed to know how well their companies were doing. With records and an accounting system, managers could report this information to the owners. However, because managers naturally want their performance to look good, there needed to be a way to ensure that the reported business information was accurate. In the United States, the Financial Accounting Standards Board (FASB) determines how accounting is practiced. The FASB works with the Securities and Exchange Commission (SEC) and the American Institute of Certified Public Accountants (AICPA), the largest professional organization of accountants.

ACCOUNTING TODAY

Computers have revolutionized accounting in the late 20th century. Tasks that are time-consuming when done by hand are handled quickly and easily by computers. Computer programs today also assist with the financial applications of accounting for easier decision-making.

The type of accounting procedure depends on the business or organization proprietorship, partnership, or corporation. A proprietorship has a single owner who is, generally, also the manager. These organizations tend to be small retail establishments or individual professional businesses. Partnerships join two or more people together as owners. Most partnerships are small or medium sized, but some are huge, exceeding 2,000 partners. A corporation is a business owned by stockholders, people who own shares in the business. A business becomes a corporation when the state approves its articles of incorporation. It becomes a legal entity, an "artificial person" that conducts business in its own name. From a legal standpoint, corporations differ significantly from proprietorships and partnerships, both of which are legally obligated for the business' debts. Accountants deal with the sublets and complexities of financial recording for businesses of all sizes.

WHAT COURSES DO YOU NEED TO TAKE?

Many universities and colleges offering a business degree will also offer an accounting emphasis. In addition to the required core curriculum of the university, which usually includes liberal arts, math, and science courses, the business department will have other requirements. The core business curriculum consists of courses in statistics, business law, finance, information systems, management, marketing, and basic accounting courses. Some universities also offer five-year professional accounting programs. The following accounting courses are usually required for the accounting emphasis, in addition to the accounting courses required in the business core:

Accounting Systems and Data Processing	Intermediate Cost Accounting
	Intermediate Financial Accounting I
Auditing	Intermediate Financial Accounting II
Income Tax Accounting	

Accounting students often specialize in a particular topical area of accounting. Examples of these specializations and recommended courses include:

- **Financial Accounting and Auditing**
  Advanced Financial Accounting
  Advanced Income Tax Accounting

- **Managerial Accounting and Systems**
  Managerial Accounting Problems and Cases
  Accounting for Government and Nonprofit Organizations

There are several fields of professional accountancy at the intermediate, advanced, and graduate levels. These courses provide preparation for practice in one or more of the following fields:

- Accounting and management control systems
- Auditing
- Financial accounting
- Managerial accounting
- Tax accounting
- Banking and Finance
- Non-profit accounting
- Teaching and research

In all of these fields, a thorough knowledge of the social, legal, economic, and political environment is needed. Courses in English composition, speech, ethics, and logic are good choices. Also, courses in statistics and information systems beyond the required business core requirements are recommended.

WHAT CAN YOU DO WITH A DEGREE IN ACCOUNTING?

Accountants are needed in almost every industry. Specifically, he could be a cost, managerial, or systems and procedures accountant. Tax, budget, and forecast accountants and auditors are also needed. An accounting degree can be used in a number of other careers. For example, in the insurance industry, with some additional training, you could be an actuary or an underwriter. You could work in the banking industry as an administrator. In financial services, people with accounting degrees are needed as financial analysts, planners, and stockbrokers. In many industries, cost estimators and compensation analysts have an accounting background.

A master's degree in business administration (MBA) helps in certain careers, such as business and public administration. By passing an inclusive exam, you could also be a Certified Public Accountant (CPA).

WHAT DO EXPERTS SAY ABOUT ACCOUNTING?

Dr. Martha Doran, Accounting Professor at San Diego State University, offers this advice to prospective students:

What can a person expect during the course of study? Students can expect some frustration and a lot of personal growth. They will also gain a good deal of discipline and logic.

What are the characteristics of a successful student? Being a strong reader is critical to success in accounting. Students will have to be able to comprehend what they read and put it in their own words. Many people think that mathematical ability is important, but if you're a good reader, that's really all you need.

What do you see for the future of the discipline? Accounting is more dynamic than it has ever been. Because there is so much information now to deal with, accountants will be required to give meaning to data. They will take all the information and determine its reliability and usefulness. There will be fewer CPAs as we have known them, and the emphasis will be on helping companies use information.

What makes this field exciting to you, personally, and why do you love what you do? Information can be very powerful—if it is applied. Company decisions are based on the interpretation of numbers. It is very interesting to take information, give meaning to it, and see decisions made based on that meaning.

BEFORE YOU DECIDE . . .

Before you invest the next four years pursuing this field of study, invest a few hours in a thorough investigation of what a degree in accounting can do for you. Use the following suggestions and the worksheet at the end of this chapter to make a plan for conducting some field research. Once your plan is complete and approved by your instructor, proceed to Part 5, Field Research, where you'll find further instructions for making the most of these activities.

TALK ABOUT IT

Conduct interviews with the following three people (using the information included in the Field Research section at the back of this book to guide your discussions):

- A senior completing a major in accounting
- An accounting professor at your school
- A professional working in an accounting-related career

READ ABOUT IT

Following is a book listing that provides an overview of possible career options for someone with a degree in accounting.

- Burnett, Rebecca. *Careers for Number Crunchers and Other Quantitative Types*. Lincolnwood, IL: VGM Career Horizons, 1993.
- Gaylord, Gloria L. *Careers in Accounting*. Lincolnwood, IL: VGM Career Horizons, 1997.
- Goldberg, Jan. *Great Jobs for Accounting Majors*. Lincolnwood, IL: NTC Publishing Group, 1998.
- Morgan, Bradley J., ed. *Business and Finance Career Directory*. Detroit: Visible Ink Press, 1993.
- Rosenthal, Lawrence. *Exploring Careers in Accounting*. New York: Rosen Publishing Group, 1993.
- Ryder, Tim. *Accounting Jobs Worldwide: A Directory of International Opportunities*. Cincinnati, OH: Seven Hills Books, 1998.

EXPERIENCE IT

Seek out an opportunity to see what a degree in accounting can do for you in the workplace. Arrange a tour, a job-shadowing experience, or even a full-fledged internship at a place such as:

- A bank
- An accounting firm
- The purchasing department of a mid-size to large corporation
- The finance office of a government agency

Once you have scheduled a first appointment, use the information included in the Field Research section of this book to make the most of this experience.

EXPLORE THE OPTIONS

Using the information included in the Field Research section at the end of this book, conduct a thorough investigation of at least two career options for college graduates with an accounting degree. You'll need a good selection of career books and resources and access to the Internet to complete this task. Here are some ways to put a degree in accounting to work. Use this list for ideas but feel free to focus your exploration on another idea that interests you.

- Actuary
- Auditor
- Banker
- Budget Officer
- Business Administrator
- Business Agent
- Certified Public Accountant
- Chief Financial Officer (CFO)
- Cost Estimator
- Financial Analyst
- Financial Planner
- Insurance Agent
- Management Consultant
- Public Administrator
- Purchasing Agent
- Stockbroker
- Tax Consultant
- Underwriter

REFERENCE

Harrison, Walter T. and Charles T. Horngren. *Financial Accounting*. Upper Saddle River, NJ: Prentice Hall, 1998.

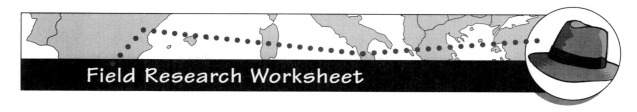

Field Research Worksheet

Now that you've learned a little about what a major in accounting is like, think about what it means for you. Could this be a good choice for you? Can you say with reasonable certainty that it's not a good fit at all? Use the following planning worksheet to explain your response.

NO WAY!

Here are three reasons why I don't think this major would be a good choice for me.

_____

_____

_____

Stop! If you are sure this is not a major you want to pursue, don't waste another minute! Move on and explore another major.

A DEFINITE MAYBE

Here are three reasons why I think this major might be a good choice for me.

_____

_____

_____

Following are my plans to find out all I can about this major.

FIELD RESEARCH PROJECT 1: TALK ABOUT IT

I will use the materials in the Field Research section of this book (Part 5) to conduct interviews with the following people:

_____ Senior completing a major in accounting

_____ Accounting professor

_____ Accounting professional

FIELD RESEARCH PROJECT 2: READ ABOUT IT

I will use Part 5 of this book to review the following book(s) about potential career tracks:

_____

_____

FIELD RESEARCH PROJECT 3: EXPERIENCE IT

I have arranged a tour or job-shadowing experience at the following location and will use Part 5 of this book to record my observations:

_____ Location

_____ Contact Person

_____ Date and Time of Appointment

FIELD RESEARCH PROJECT 4: EXPLORE THE OPTIONS

I want to find out all I can about the following career(s) and will use Part 5 of this book to guide my investigation at the library and on the Internet:

_____ Career Choice #1

_____ Career Choice #2

_____

Student's Name and Date

_____ Field Research Plan Approved
_____ Field Research Plan Not Approved

Because:

_____

_____

_____

Instructor's Signature and Date

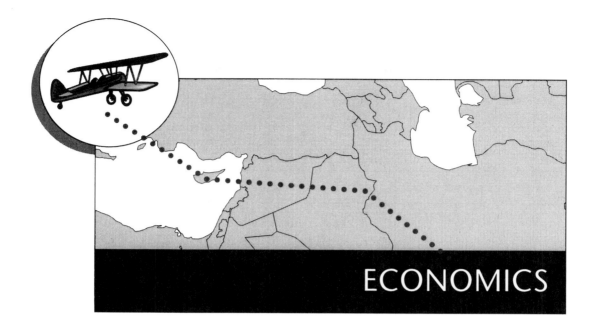

ECONOMICS

Is This Major for You?

- Do you typically keep track of whether it's a bull or bear market and almost always know what the current GNP (gross national product) is?
- Do you have strong opinions one way or the other about Adam Smith's economic philosophy as expressed in the classic "Wealth of Nations"?
- Do you think that you'd enjoying pursuing a course of study with a heavy mix of math, history, and logic?
- Is it important that you understand why things happen and that you have a part in making positive changes?
- Are you able to visualize the "big picture" as well as all the little details in a given situation?
- Does the prospect of dealing with issues such as finances, supply and demand, and economic forecasts appeal to you?
- Does having the financial well-being of other people or even entire nations resting on your shoulders sound like a challenge you'd like to handle?

If you answered yes to several of these questions, keep reading and find out if a degree in economics is a good choice for you.

INTRODUCTION

Did you know that with a college degree, your starting salary may be about 80% higher than that of a high school graduate and about 10 times higher than the salary in a typical developing nation? Why does the unemployment rate vary

Dr. Art O'Sullivan, Economics Professor at Oregon State University, contributed to this article.

from year to year? Will this affect your career decision? When we make a career choice, buy a new car, or listen to the news reports about inflation and unemployment rates, we see the influence of economics. If you are curious to find answers to how the world works, economics may be for you!

WHAT IS ECONOMICS?

Economics is the study of how people make choices when faced with scarcity. Because resources—time, money, land, water—are limited, we must make difficult choices about how we will spend them. For example, if we buy a less expensive car, we might be able to afford a needed computer. Economics is the study of choices on an individual, national, and global level. The principles of economics influence decisions that affect the well-being of people around the world. With the help of economics, we can understand the world and make better decisions for our lives.

HISTORY AND BACKGROUND

Early economic theories were based on the principle that government should regulate economic activities because only government could ensure that trade was conducted fairly. In the 1700s, the idea emerged that government should participate less in economic life. The writings of Adam Smith (1723–1790) advocated free competition and free trade as a way to promote economic growth. His book, *An Inquiry into the Nature and Causes of the Wealth of Nations* (published in 1776), provided the foundation for the free enterprise system and contains insights that guide modern economic analysis.

Smith argued that human progress is possible in a society where individuals follow their own self-interests, and this individualism leads to social order and progress. In order to make money, people produce things that other people are willing to buy. Buyers spend money for things they need or want most. When buyers and sellers meet in the market, a natural pattern of production develops that produces social harmony. Smith also believed that national income grows when profits are used to expand production, which creates more and more jobs and national prosperity. He advocated that governments stay out of business and provide only social needs not met by the market.

In the early 1900s, economists began to apply the scientific method to the study of economic problems. They studied the booms and depressions associated with free enterprise, and they discovered specific relationships between different aspects of the economy.

ECONOMICS TODAY

Today the field of economics is studied from two perspectives: microeconomics and macroeconomics. Microeconomics is the study of the choices that are made by individuals, firms, and government and how these choices affect the markets for all sorts of goods and services. Through microeconomic analysis, we can (1) understand how markets work, (2) make personal and managerial decisions, and (3) evaluate the merits of public policies.

Macroeconomics is the study of the nation's economy as a whole. Macroeconomics is a policy-oriented subject that was developed as a separate subject during the 1930s when the entire world suffered from massive unemployment. Through macroeconomic analysis, we can (1) understand how a national economy works, (2) understand the debates over economic policy, and (3) make informed business decisions on a global scale.

WHAT COURSES DO YOU NEED TO TAKE?

Many universities offering a bachelor of arts degree in economics require some of the following courses:

History of Economic Thought	Principles of Macroeconomics
Intermediate Macroeconomics	Principles of Microeconomics
Intermediate Microeconomics	Statistics
Introduction to Econometrics	

Elective courses are usually offered in areas such as:

Economic Development	International Trade and Finance
Economic Forecasting	Labor Economics
Environmental Economics	Money and Banking
Industrial Organization	

If you are considering an advanced degree in economics, it is very important to take several advanced courses in mathematics.

WHAT CAN YOU DO WITH A DEGREE IN ECONOMICS?

Economists are needed in many industries and can apply their knowledge in a number of careers. In the insurance industry, economic majors are hired to be actuaries and underwriters. Because they understand the interactions of many economic variables and policies, economists are needed in the financial industry as bank administrators, financial analysts, and investor relations managers.

Economists, working in other types of business and public utilities, spend much of their time applying economic theory to analyze issues that are important to their firm. They may analyze the effects of economic activity in the U.S. and the world, on demand for the company's product, conduct a cost-benefit analysis of projects that the company is considering, or determine the effects of government regulations on the company. Careers in these areas include compensation analyst, business administrator, market researcher, and cost estimator.

Economists in governmental agencies may forecast the effects of various policy proposals on the economy and study the impacts of governmental regulations and taxes on industries. Economists in international development and trade are especially needed. The governmental sector also needs regional planners, demographers, and statisticians.

Research and university teaching are open to individuals with master's and doctoral degrees. Economics also provides a very good basis for entering law school.

BEFORE YOU DECIDE . . .

Before you invest the next four years pursuing this field of study, invest a few hours in a thorough investigation of what a degree in economics can do for you. Use the following suggestions and the worksheet at the end of this chapter to make a plan for conducting some field research. Once your plan is complete and approved by your instructor, proceed to Part 5, Field Research, where you'll find further instructions for making the most of these activities.

TALK ABOUT IT

Conduct interviews with the following three people (using the information included in the Field Research section in Part 5 of this book to guide your discussions):

- A senior completing a major in economics
- An economics professor at your school
- A professional working in an economics-related career

READ ABOUT IT

Following is a book listing that provides an overview of possible career options for someone with a degree in economics.

- *Career Choices: Economics*. New York: Walker, 1985.
- Fischgrund, Tom. *The Insider's Guide to the Top 20 Careers in Business and Management: What's It's Really Like to Work in Advertising, Computers, Banking, Management, and More*. New York: McGraw-Hill, 1994.
- Hamadeh, H.S. and Andy Richard. *Business School Companion: The Ultimate Guide to Excelling in Business School and Launching Your Career*. New York: Random House, 1995.
- *Job Opportunities for Business Graduates*. Princeton, NJ: Peterson's, 1995.
- Mayall, Donald. *Careers in Banking and Finance*. Washington, D. C.: American Institute of Banking, 1997.
- Morgan, Bradley J., ed. *Business and Finance Career Directory*. Detroit: Visible Ink Press, 1993.
- Naficy, Mariam. *The Fast Track: The Insider's Guide to Winning Jobs in Management, Consulting, Investment Banking, and Security Trading*. NY: Broadway Books, 1997.
- Wallace, Chris D. *Finance Career Guide 1998*. Boston: Harvard Business School Publishing, 1997.

EXPERIENCE IT

Seek out an opportunity to see what a degree in economics can do for you in the workplace. Arrange a tour, a job-shadowing experience, or even a full-fledged internship at a place such as:

- A bank
- A stock exchange
- A stock brokerage firm
- A federal agency
- A publisher of financial information
- An insurance agency

Once you have scheduled a first appointment, use the information included in the Field Research section of this book to make the most of this experience.

EXPLORE THE OPTIONS

Using the materials included in the Field Research section at the end of this book, conduct a thorough investigation of at least two career options for college graduates with an economics degree. You'll need a good selection of career books and resources and access to the Internet to complete this task.

Here are some ways to put a degree in economics to work. Use this list for ideas but feel free to focus your exploration on another idea that interests you.

- Actuary
- Attorney
- Banker
- Business Administrator
- Business Journalist
- College Professor
- Compensation Analyst
- Cost Estimator
- Demographer
- Diplomat
- Financial Analyst
- International Trade Specialist
- Investment Banker
- Investor Relations Manager
- Market Researcher
- Policy Analyst
- Public Administrator
- Regional Planner
- Statistician
- Stockbroker
- Teacher (K–12)
- Underwriter

REFERENCE

O'Sullivan, Arthur and Steven M. Sheffrin. *Micro Economics: Princples and Tools*. Upper Saddle River, NJ: Prentice Hall, 1997.

Now that you've learned a little about what a major in economics is like, think about what it means for you. Could this be a good choice for you? Can you say with reasonable certainty that it's not a good fit at all? Use the following planning worksheet to explain your response.

NO WAY!

Here are three reasons why I don't think this major would be a good choice for me.

_____

_____

_____

Stop! If you are sure this is not a major you want to pursue, don't waste another minute! Move on and explore another major.

A DEFINITE MAYBE

Here are three reasons why I think this major might be a good choice for me.

_____

_____

_____

Following are my plans to find out all I can about this major.

FIELD RESEARCH PROJECT 1: TALK ABOUT IT

I will use the materials included in the Field Research section of this book (Part 5) to conduct interviews with the following people:

_____ Senior completing a major in economics

_____ Economics professor

_____ Economics professional

FIELD RESEARCH PROJECT 2: READ ABOUT IT

I will use the materials included in the Field Research section of this book to review the following book(s) about potential career tracks:

_____

_____

Field Research Worksheet

FIELD RESEARCH PROJECT 3: EXPERIENCE IT

I have arranged a tour or job-shadowing experience at the following location and will use the materials included in Part 5 of this book to record my observations:

_____ Location

_____ Contact Person

_____ Date and Time of Appointment

FIELD RESEARCH PROJECT 4: EXPLORE THE OPTIONS

I want to find out all I can about the following career(s) and will use the materials included in the Part 5 of this book to guide my investigation at the library and on the Internet:

_____ Career Choice #1

_____ Career Choice #2

. . . .

_____

Student's Name and Date

_____ Field Research Plan Approved

_____ Field Research Plan Not Approved

Because:

_____

_____

_____

Instructor's Signature and Date

. . . .

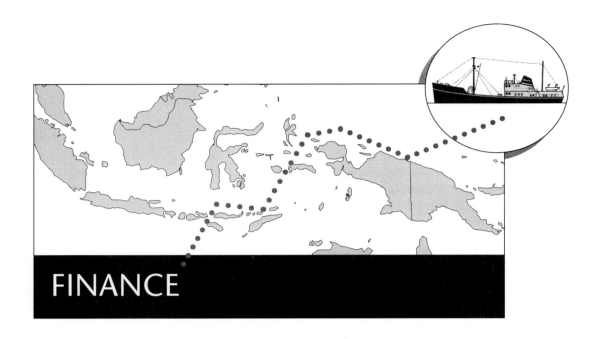

FINANCE

Is This Major for You?

- Have you ever served as treasurer of a club or sports team and actually enjoyed the job?
- Are you good at maintaining a personal budget (at least on paper)?
- Do you enjoy following the stock market?
- Do you like to dabble in stocks and bonds (even if it is on a very small scale)?
- Are you detail-oriented, precise, and dependable?
- Are you good at keeping secrets?
- Do you consider your people skills a strong suit?

If you answered yes to several of these questions, keep reading to find out if a finance major is a good choice for you.

INTRODUCTION

Do you know that if someone invested $1,000 for 400 years at 8% interest, it would grow to $23 quadrillion—that's roughly $5 million per person on Earth. Wow! Benjamin Franklin had a good understanding of the time value of money when he left $1,000 to Boston. Two hundred years later, Franklin's gift, after much of it was used for humanitarian efforts, is still worth over $3 million. When you save money or when you borrow it from a bank to finance a new stereo or your college education, you are using the country's financial market system. If you are interested in understanding and applying these principles to create and maintain wealth, finance could be for you!

Dr. Art Keown, Finance Professor at Virginia Polytechnic Institute, contributed to this article.

WHAT IS FINANCE?

Finance is the study of how to create and maintain wealth. It is the art of administering and managing money that is crucial to the success of every business. Although you learn and use many calculations, financial management is really concerned with the logic behind the calculations. For instance, finance deals with the factors that determine interest rates and the effects of those rates on future earnings. It assesses the valuation and characteristics of stocks and bonds and how to evaluate a firm's financial performance. It examines the functions and purposes of monetary systems, credit, prices, money markets, and financial institutions.

HISTORY AND BACKGROUND

Before money existed, people produced much of what they needed to live and traded for items they could not produce themselves. When only real, tangible assets existed, people could save only those items. This is inconvenient, at best, and provides no mechanism to transfer the savings for value.

When coins and currency were created, people could then compile savings in the form of money. This was better, but not perfect, because there was still no mechanism to transfer money. Very few people just hand over their cash! The concept of a receipt that represented the transfer of savings from one economic unit to another moved the system further along. Receipts enabled a person or organization that had surplus savings to lend those savings and earn a rate of return from the borrower. Loan brokers located excess savings and channeled them to people needing funds. Sometimes people purchased the financial claims of the borrowers and sold them at a higher price to other investors. This process is called underwriting. In addition, secondary markets developed, which traded in already existing financial claims.

In advanced financial market systems, financial intermediaries come into existence. These are the major financial institutions, such as banks, savings and loan associations, credit unions, life insurance companies, and mutual funds. They each offer their own financial claims, called indirect securities, for entities with excess savings. The proceeds from selling these indirect securities are used to purchase the financial claims of others, the direct securities. For example, a mutual fund company sells its own shares (indirect securities) and buys common stock from other corporations (direct securities). A developed financial market system provides for a greater level of wealth in the economy.

FINANCE TODAY

The field of finance has undergone a change over the past decade because of the wave of acquisitions, mergers, and divestitures. The United States Department of Labor Statistics estimates that financial services will grow at a faster rate than services as a whole. With this growth comes a lot of controversy and debate about the system's alterations. Since late 1986, there has been a renewal of public interest in the regulation of the country's financial markets. Stock market scandal and the collapse of the equity markets on October 19, 1987, when the Dow Jones Industrial Average fell by an unprecedented 508 points, contribute to the system's insecurity. More recently, in early 1990, the investing community became increasingly concerned over a weakening in the so-called junk bond market. Finally, in 1998, concern about struggling foreign markets began another period of instability. With all of this new awareness has come an appreciation of the crucial role that regulation plays in the financial system.

WHAT COURSES DO YOU NEED TO TAKE?

Many universities and colleges require a core curriculum of liberal arts, science, and math designed to increase overall knowledge. Generally, business schools require additional core courses. Many universities offer an emphasis in finance, and minors in this subject are also available at some universities. The following courses are usually required for a finance emphasis in addition to finance courses in the business core:

> Corporate Financial Decisions
> Financial Markets and Institutions
> International Financial Management
> Investment and Portfolio Management

> Accounting courses are also recommended.

WHAT CAN YOU DO WITH A DEGREE IN FINANCE?

There are four basic career areas in finance:

> Banking
> Consumer Credit
> Corporate Finance
> Securities

In the banking sector, positions for finance majors include commercial loan officer, consumer bank officer, trust administrator, and bank manager. There are opportunities with the Federal Reserve Bank as examiners and operations analysts. In the consumer credit area, jobs related to installment cash, sales, and mortgage credit are available, as well as consumer credit counselors and credit officers and managers.

In corporate finance, the chief financial officer is at the top of the ladder. Other positions include treasurer, controller, pension fund manager, financial analyst, or financial public relations. Securities sales and trading, as well as financial planning and underwriting, need finance majors. The SEC hires people with finance degrees as investigators.

Becoming a CPA or earning an MBA can help to secure a job in some of these fields. There is also a growing availability of positions in international finance.

WHAT DO EXPERTS SAY ABOUT FINANCE?

Dr. Art Keown, Finance Professor at Virginia Polytechnic Institute, offers this advice to prospective students:

What can a person expect during the course of study? During their study of finance, students should expect to focus on decision-making, to use analytical skills, discover how to value assets, and propose projects.

What are the characteristics of a successful student? In this major, especially, students need to keep up with their homework. They must be willing to do all of the problems assigned because the topics build upon themselves. The math is not difficult, but the only way to learn is to be committed to doing the work.

What do you see for the future of the discipline? Years ago there were distinct borders between countries. In the future, however, we will continue to see less of that. The flow of money comes from all over the world, and the field has become much more global. We will be dealing with more risk associated with currency conversion and will see many more U.S. companies operating outside the United States.

What makes this field exciting to you, personally, and why do you love what you do? There is real applicability to finance. It focuses on how to make logical decisions and has relevance to everyone. Many people cannot rely on a pension or retirement fund from their company and are investing for themselves. Every night I have a new take on what's going on when I watch the stock market. It affects me, as well as my field. Everyone is interested in the market. If they have money in it, they want to see it grow. Even if they don't have money in it, they're still interested because they want to see it decline so that everyone else loses their money! Either way, everyone is interested.

BEFORE YOU DECIDE . . .

Before you invest the next four years pursuing this field of study, invest a few hours in a thorough investigation of what a degree in finance can do for you. Use the following suggestions and the worksheet at the end of this chapter to make a plan for conducting some field research. Once your plan is complete and approved by your instructor, proceed to Part 5, Field Research, where you'll find further instructions for making the most of these activities.

TALK ABOUT IT

Conduct interviews with the following three people (using the information included in the Field Research section in Part 5 of this book to guide your discussion):

- A senior completing a degree in finance
- A finance professor at your school
- A professional working in a finance career

READ ABOUT IT

Following is a book listing that provides an overview of possible career options for someone with a degree in finance.

- Crist, Dean. *Opportunities in Financial Careers*. Lincolnwood, IL: VGM Career Horizons, 1991.
- Haddock, Patricia. *Careers in Banking and Finance*. New York: Rosen Publishing Group, 1997.
- Hunt, Christopher W. *Job Seeker's Guide to Wall Street Recruiters*. New York: John Wiley & Sons, 1998.
- *Job Opportunities for Business Majors*. Princeton, NJ: Peterson's, 1998.
- Naficy, Mariam. *The Insider's Guide to Winning Jobs in Management Consulting, Investment Banking and Securities Trading*. NY: Broadway Books, 1997
- Ring, Trudy. *Careers in Finance*. Lincolnwood, IL: VGM Career Horizons, 1997.
- Stair, Lila B. *Careers in Business*. Lincolnwood, IL: VGM Career Horizons, 1991.
- Wallace, Chris D. *Finance Career Guide*. Boston: Harvard Business School Publishing, 1998.

EXPERIENCE IT

Seek out an opportunity to see what a degree in finance can do for you in the workplace. Arrange a tour, a job-shadowing experience, or even a full-fledged internship at a place such as:

- A bank
- An investment firm
- A credit bureau
- A mortgage company
- A venture capital investment firm

Once you have scheduled a first appointment, use the information included in the Field Research section of this book to make the most of this experience.

EXPLORE THE OPTIONS

Using the materials included in the Field Research section at the end of this book, conduct a thorough investigation of at least two career options for college graduates with a finance degree. You'll need a good selection of career books and resources and access to the Internet to complete this task. Here are some ways to put a degree in finance to work. Use this list for ideas but feel free to focus your exploration on another idea that interests you.

- Accountant
- Actuary
- Auditor
- Banker
- Benefits Officer
- Budget Officer

- Business Administrator
- Business Agent
- Chief Financial Officer
- Controller
- Cost Estimator
- Credit Manager
- Financial Analyst
- Financial Planner
- Insurance Agent

- Investor
- Management Consultant
- Mortgage Banker
- Public Administrator
- Purchasing Agent
- Stockbroker
- Treasurer
- Underwriter

REFERENCE

Keown, Arthur. *Personal Finance: Turning Money Into Wealth*. Upper Saddle River, NJ: Prentice Hall, 1998.

Now that you've learned a little about what a major in finance is like, think about what it means for you. Could this be a good choice? Can you say with reasonable certainty that it's not a good fit at all? Use the following planning worksheet to explain your response.

NO WAY!

Here are three reasons why I don't think this major would be a good choice for me.

_____

_____

_____

Stop! If you are sure this is not a major you want to pursue, don't waste another minute! Move on and explore another major.

A DEFINITE MAYBE

Here are three reasons why I think this major might be a good choice for me.

_____

_____

_____

Following are my plans to find out all I can about this major.

FIELD RESEARCH PROJECT 1: TALK ABOUT IT

I will use the materials included in the Field Research section of this book (Part 5) to conduct interviews with the following people:

_____ Senior completing a major in finance

_____ Finance professor

_____ Finance professional

FIELD RESEARCH PROJECT 2: READ ABOUT IT

I will use the materials included in Part 5 of this book to review the following book(s) about potential career tracks:

_____

_____

FIELD RESEARCH PROJECT 3: EXPERIENCE IT

I have arranged a tour or job-shadowing experience at the following locations and will use the materials included in Part 5 of this book to record my observations:

_____ Location

_____ Contact Person

_____ Date and Time of Appointment

FIELD RESEARCH PROJECT 4: EXPLORE THE OPTIONS

I want to find out all I can about the following career(s) and will use the materials included in Part 5 of this book to guide my investigation at the library and on the Internet:

_____ Career Choice #1

_____ Career Choice #2

_____

Student's Name and Date

_____ Field Research Plan Approved

_____ Field Research Plan Not Approved

Because:

_____

_____

_____

Instructor's Signature and Date

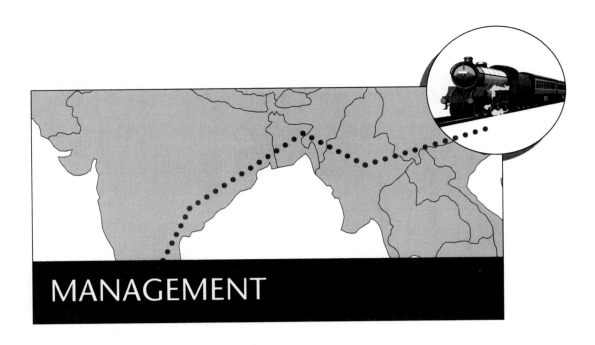

MANAGEMENT

Is This Major for You?

- Have you ever participated in student government or been chosen to lead a school club or sports team?
- Are you the one others count on to plan a great party or organize impromptu outings with a group of friends?
- Do you plan each day and keep track of it on a calendar?
- Are you well-organized?
- Do you tend to keep lists of things to do?
- Are you a good note-taker?
- Are you someone who enjoys being around people a lot?
- Are you pretty good at mediating disagreements among friends?
- Does working in a fast-paced, competitive business environment appeal to you?

If you answered yes to several of these questions, keep reading and find out if a major in management is a good choice for you.

INTRODUCTION

Imagine that you're the president of a very successful company. What kinds of things are you doing? Do you spend your time "wining and dining" clients? Are you concerned with motivating your employees to do their best? Do you spend a lot of time networking with people? What exactly is it that makes a manager

Dr. Gary Dessler, Management Professor at Florida International University, contributed to this article.

successful? The study of management answers this question, but successful management is a work in progress, and it takes a business lifetime to really understand how to manage. If you see yourself dedicated to making a company and the people in that company successful, management may be a good career choice for you.

WHAT IS MANAGEMENT?

Management is the process of accomplishing goals, or sets of goals, with and through other people. There are different types of managers depending on their experience—first-line managers (supervisors), middle managers, and top managers, but they all perform the following four basic functions:

PLANNING. Setting goals and deciding on courses of action, developing rules and procedures, developing plans, and forecasting what the future will likely be for the firm.

ORGANIZING. Entails identifying jobs to be done, hiring people to do them, establishing departments, delegating authority to subordinates, establishing a chain of command, and coordinating the work of the manager's subordinates.

LEADING. Motivating other people to get the job done, maintaining morale, modeling company culture, and managing conflicts and communication.

CONTROLLING. Setting standards (such as sales quotas or quality standards), comparing actual performance with these standards, and taking corrective action as needed.

Managers do not spend an equal amount of time on each function. Usually, top managers will spend more of their time planning, while first-line managers use most of their time leading and controlling. Through an understanding of general management principles, individual and group behavior, organizational change and design, and human resources management, managers can make an impact on the success of an organization.

HISTORY AND BACKGROUND

Management is a very old idea. Hunters used it when they formed tribes for protection; the Egyptians used it to build pyramids; and the Romans used it to control their empire. Management theory as we know it today began with an effort to study the management process with scientific rigor. This began in the mid-1700s with the birth of the Industrial Revolution. The division and specialization of work led to enormous increases in productivity and output. Frank Taylor developed a set of principles that became known as "scientific management," which meant that managers should scientifically determine the best way to get the job done.

Scientific management became very popular but eventually scrutinized every detail of the work process in such depth that the individual's needs were ignored. In 1927, Chicago's Hawthorne Plant of the Western Electric Company conducted what became known as the Hawthorne Studies. The original study focused on employee working conditions. It looked at the effect of lighting on productivity—low, medium, and bright light. What they found surprised everyone at the time. No matter what they did, productivity increased. They concluded that the researcher's interaction with the employees during the study made them feel special and resulted in the productivity increase, and so began the human relations movement and behavioral approach to management. Behavior scientists like Douglas McGregor and Rensis Likert translated their ideas into methodologies that became the basis for partcipative management and management by objectives (MBO), where subordinates set their goals with their supervisors and are measured on the accomplishment of these goals.

MANAGEMENT TODAY

After World War II, a trend of applying quantitative techniques to a wide range of managerial problems developed. This movement, management science, like scientific management, uses the scientific method to find the best solution to industrial problems. This approach is closely associated with the systems approach, which views an organization as a system made up of different, interrelated parts. Since the 1960s, organizations have started using the contingency approach to management—changing the management principles and organizational structure based on the rate of change in an organization's environment and technology. Successful managers today cultivate three processes aimed at getting the company's employees to focus their attention on creating change. They are:

THE ENTREPRENEURIAL PROCESS. Entrepreneurs are people who start their own businesses. Employees who have authority, support, and success-related rewards can also act as if they own the operations they are managing.

THE COMPETENCE-BUILDING PROCESS. Successful managers take advantage of the talents and knowledge of their employees. They devote much of their efforts to creating an environment that encourages employees to take on more responsibility and providing the education and training employees need to build their self-confidence.

THE RENEWAL PROCESS. Employees should be encouraged to develop the habit of questioning why things are done as they are and whether it might not be better to disrupt the status quo and do things differently. This helps to guard against complacency.

WHAT COURSES DO YOU NEED TO TAKE?

Many universities and colleges offering a business degree will also offer a management emphasis. In addition to the required core curriculum of the university, which usually includes liberal arts, math, and science courses, the business department will have other requirements. The core business curriculum consists of courses in accounting, statistics, business law, finance, information systems, marketing, and management. The following courses are usually required for a management emphasis in addition to management courses in the business core:

Labor and Employee Relations

Introduction to International Business

Human Resources Management: Compensation Administration

Special Topics in Management

There are specialty areas in management, such as hotel, hospital, airport, and city management, that require additional course work.

WHAT CAN YOU DO WITH A DEGREE IN MANAGEMENT?

A degree in business administration prepares you for a wide range of jobs in accounting, sales, production, and management. Although recent graduates do not go into high-level management positions immediately, there are various paths that will lead to these positions. Many industries look for graduates with management degrees for supervisory positions (if he has a knowledge of the industry). If he chooses to go into the banking or financial services industries, he can begin a career as an administrator, bank loan officer, or investor relations manager. Financial analysts and planners, management consultants, purchasing agents, sales agents, salespeople, and information specialists are needed in many industries. With additional training, he can also go into hotel, airport, city, or hospital management. A master's degree in business administration in conjunction with work experience can sometimes help to further your career into upper-level management.

WHAT DO EXPERTS SAY ABOUT MANAGEMENT?

Dr. Gary Dessler, Management Professor at Florida International University, offers this advice to prospective students:

What can a person expect during the course of study? Managers are people who get things done through others, so you'll learn how to work with other people and motivate them.

What are the characteristics of a successful student? They enjoy working with and influencing other people. Successful students are also analytical and are somewhat political—they learn how to work with "office politics."

What do you see for the future of the discipline? Between now and the year 2004, availability of jobs for managers will grow at a faster rate than that of any other field, according to the Department of Labor Statistics. Managers will be needed in almost every industry, from hospital administrator to police chief.

What makes the field exciting to you, personally, and why do you love what you do? Building a business by working with and through other people is challenging and rewarding. To see the growth of an organization and its effect on society and the employees can be very satisfying.

BEFORE YOU DECIDE . . .

Before you invest the next four years pursuing this field of study, invest a few hours in a thorough investigation of what a degree in management can do for you. Use the following suggestions and the worksheet at the end of this chapter to make a plan for conducting some field research. Once your plan is complete and approved by your instructor, proceed to Part 5, Field Research, where you'll find further instructions for making the most of these activities.

TALK ABOUT IT

Conduct interviews with the following three people (using the information included in the Field Research section in Part 5 of this book to guide your discussions):

- A senior completing a degree in management
- A management professor at your school
- A professional working in a management-related career

READ ABOUT IT

Following is a book listing that provides an overview of possible career options for someone with a degree in management.

- Beatty, Richard H. *The Executive's Career Guide: Inside Advice on Getting to the Top from Today's Business Leaders*. New York: John Wiley & Sons, 1995.
- Butler, Timothy and James Waldroop. *Discovering Your Career In Business*. New York: Addison-Wesley, 1997.
- Camenson, Blythe. *Careers for Self-Starters and Other Entrepreneurial Types*. Lincolnwood, IL: VGM Career Horizons, 1997.
- Farr, J. Michael. *America's Top Office, Management, Sales and Professional Jobs*. Indianapolis: JIST Works, 1996.
- Fischgrund, Tom. *The Insider's Guide to the Top 20 Careers in Business Management*. New York: McGraw-Hill, 1994.
- Granrose, Cherlyn Shromme. *The Careers of Business Managers in East Asia*. Westport, CT: Greenwood Publishing Group, 1997.
- *Job Choices in Business*. Bethlehem, PA: National Association of Colleges and Employers, 1998.
- *Job Opportunities for Business Majors*. Princeton, NJ: Peterson's, 1998.
- Kivirst, Lisa. *Kiss Off Corporate America: A Young Professional's Guide to Independence*. Kansas City, MO: Andrews McMeel Publishing, 1998.
- Naficy, Mariam. *The Insider's Guide to Winning Jobs in Management Consulting, Investment Banking and Securities Trading*. New York: Broadway Books, 1997.
- Osterman, Paul. *Broken Ladders: Managerial Careers in the New Economy*. New York: Oxford University Press, 1996.

EXPERIENCE IT

Seek out an opportunity to see what a degree in management can do for you in the workplace. Arrange a tour, a job-shadowing experience, or even a full-fledged internship at a place such as:

- A large corporate headquarters
- A self-employed management consultant
- A military unit
- A small or mid-size company
- A government agency

Once you have scheduled a first appointment, use the information included in the Field Research section of this book to make the most of this experience.

EXPLORE THE OPTIONS

Using the materials included in the Field Research section at the end of this book, conduct a thorough investigation of at least two career options for college graduates with a management degree. You'll need a good selection of career books and resources and access to the Internet to complete this task. Here are some ways to put a degree in management to work. Use this list for ideas but feel free to focus your exploration on another idea that interests you.

- Accountant
- Banker
- Business Administrator
- Chief Executive Officer (CEO)
- Development Director
- Economist
- Entrepreneur
- Financial Analyst
- Financial Planner
- Lawyer
- Management Consultant
- Manager (business, industry, retail, manufacturing, entertainment, etc.)
- Managing Editor
- Nonprofit Agency Director
- Purchasing Agent
- Stockbroker
- Trainer

REFERENCE

Dessler, Gary. *Management: Leading People and Organizations Into the 21st Century*. Upper Saddle River, NJ: Prentice Hall, 1998.

Now that you've learned a little about what a major in management is like, think about what it means for you. Could this be a good choice? Can you say with reasonable certainty that it's not a good fit at all? Use the following planning worksheet to explain your response.

NO WAY!

Here are three reasons why I don't think this major would be a good choice for me.

_____

_____

_____

Stop! If you are sure this is not a major you want to pursue, don't waste another minute! Move on and explore another major.

A DEFINITE MAYBE

Here are three reasons why I think this major might be a good choice for me.

_____

_____

_____

Following are my plans to find out all I can about this major.

FIELD RESEARCH PROJECT 1: TALK ABOUT IT

I will use the materials included in the Field Research section of this book (Part 5) to conduct interviews with the following people:

_____ Senior completing a major in management

_____ Management professor

_____ Management professional

FIELD RESEARCH PROJECT 2: READ ABOUT IT

I will use the materials included in Part 5 of this book to review the following book(s) about potential career tracks:

_____

_____

Field Research Worksheet

FIELD RESEARCH PROJECT 3: EXPERIENCE IT

I have arranged a tour or job-shadowing experience at the following location and will use the materials included in Part 5 of this book to record my observations:

_____ Location

_____ Contact Person

_____ Date and Time of Appointment

FIELD RESEARCH PROJECT 4: EXPLORE THE OPTIONS

I want to find out all I can about the following career(s) and will use the materials included in Part 5 of this book to guide my investigation at the library and on the Internet:

_____ Career Choice #1

_____ Career Choice #2

· ·

_____

Student's Name and Date

_____ Field Research Plan Approved
_____ Field Research Plan Not Approved

Because:

_____

_____

_____

Instructor's Signature and Date

· ·

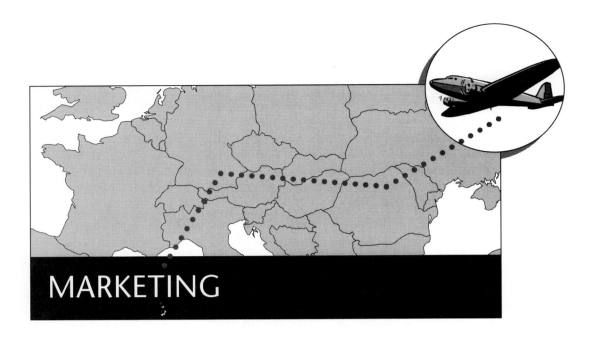

MARKETING

Is This Major for You?

- Has anyone ever told you that you are a natural-born saleperson?
- Did you enjoy getting involved in school fundraisers?
- Did you ever run your own lemonade stand, have a newspaper route, or find other ways to earn money as a child?
- Do you have a knack for persuading others to share your point of view?
- Are the commercials one of your favorite parts of television viewing?
- Can you sing, word for word, the jingles from countless advertising campaigns?
- Are you interested in communicating exciting ideas about various products and programs to the public?

If you answered yes to several of these questions, keep reading to find out if a major in marketing is a good choice for you.

INTRODUCTION

What do the type of jeans you wear say about you? There are many jeans styles to choose from—how do you decide which is right for you? Every day we are exposed to hundreds of products and make as many decisions about which to buy. The specific way a need is satisfied depends on the individual. For example, two classmates may feel their stomachs rumbling during a lunchtime

Dr. Joel Evans and Dr. Barry Berman, Marketing Professors at Hofstra University, contributed to this article.

lecture and feel an intense need for food. However, the way each person goes about satisfying this need might be quite different. The first person may be a health nut who fantasizes about gulping down a big handful of trail mix, while the second person may be equally aroused by the prospect of a greasy cheeseburger and fries. Marketers often go to great lengths to influence the decisions that consumers make. If you are interested in what motivates people and how companies can provide products for different groups, marketing may be the field for you!

WHAT IS MARKETING?

Marketing is the study of the relationship between what customers want and need and the products or services needed to meet those wants and needs. It sounds simple, but in today's business environment there are actually many functions of marketing that companies must perform in order to succeed. Behind the scenes, businesses must analyze external factors, such as the economy, competition, and trends, and determine consumer characteristics and needs before they begin planning the products themselves. The product that eventually is offered goes through a number of modifications. Decisions have been made on everything from the images and brand name to packaging and optional features. Communicating with customers and the public through advertising, public relations, personal selling, and sales promotions is another important part of the marketing process. The price and distribution process must also be determined. Marketing managers coordinate all of these functions in order to make a product or service successful. It definitely takes more than just a good idea!

HISTORY AND BACKGROUND

Did you ever trade your Coca-Cola for a Hershey bar? If so, you engaged in the earliest form of marketing, barter. Before people had money, they had to trade for anything that they could not produce themselves. Over time, some people became better at certain jobs. Those who were hunters traded pelts and meat for the food grown by the farmer. One farmer's potatoes could be traded for another's wheat. Indeed, the barter system is still practiced in many parts of the world. Eventually, there were so many exchanges that trading posts, traveling salespeople, stores, and cities evolved. A standardized monetary system was then developed that made exchanges much easier.

The modern system of marketing began with industrialization. Mass production and specialization enabled people to turn from self-sufficient living to purchasing many of their needs. When production became so efficient that a large quantity of products could be produced, firms hired sales forces and used advertising in an attempt to make people want their products. Firms produced a lot of products and tried to convince consumers to buy them without determining anything about the wants and needs of the market. However, as competition grew, and there was more supply than demand, firms realized that it was necessary to investigate the market before creating the product.

MARKETING TODAY

In competitive industries today, most company decisions are made with the customer in mind. To be competitive on a global scale in business today, firms need to know and quickly react to people's desires and motivations. After their research is done, the company's marketing program can be planned and carried out in an integrated manner. As marketers determine the best way to present goods or services for consumer consideration, they have a number of decisions to make. The marketer's strategic toolbox is called the marketing mix, which consists of factors that can be combined and manipulated to create a desired response in the marketplace. These factors are the product itself, the price of the product, the place where it is made available, and the promotion that makes it known to consumers.

WHAT COURSES DO YOU NEED TO TAKE?

Many universities and colleges offering a business degree will also offer a marketing emphasis. A minor in marketing is also possible at many universities. The core business curriculum consists of courses in accounting, statistics, business law, finance, information systems, management, and basic marketing courses. Requirements for the marketing emphasis or marketing minor usually will include three or more of the following:

Advertising Management and Public Relations	Marketing Strategy and Policy
	Sales Management
Business Marketing	Personal Selling
Buyer Behavior	Physical Distribution Management
International Advertising	Product Strategy
International Marketing	Transportation
Marketing Analysis	

Many marketing positions require computer skills, and some firms value courses that are applicable to their industry.

WHAT CAN YOU DO WITH A DEGREE IN MARKETING?

Because marketing is an essential part of business today, there are a great number of career opportunities in many industries that are open to graduating students with marketing degrees. Many types of sales representative entry-level positions exist in many industries, which include advertising sales, direct sales, business-to-business sales, retail sales, and sales management. Besides sales, marketing majors can seek careers as brand, marketing, promotion, and product managers. Other positions for marketing majors in advertising include advertising copywriter and media director. Public relations, marketing research analyst, or research at the university level with an advanced degree are other career paths in which a marketing degree can be beneficial.

WHAT DO EXPERTS SAY ABOUT MARKETING?

Dr. Mike Solomon, Marketing Professor at Auburn University, offers this advice to prospective students:

What can a person expect during the course of study? Marketing is changing so rapidly that even marketing professors cannot project what their courses will be two to four years from now. Marketing integrates concepts from economics, psychology, and sociology, among others, to teach efficient management and responsible analysis of industry trends. Marketing is fun and provides an opportunity to look at daily life in a fundamental way—to recognize the "signs" of marketing that surround you, from glittering products in colorful packages to long-term service programs, designed for you and your family.

What are the characteristics of a successful student? Marketing is both an art and a science. The successful student needs to be able to understand both aspects, from crunching numbers to imagining new ways to describe an intangible idea. Most of all, she needs to be open-minded and able to grasp the "big picture"—to understand how the different aspects of marketing must fit together to serve the needs of the customer and create value for the organization and for society.

What do you see for the future of the discipline? As we continue the transition to a service-oriented economy, opportunities continue to multiply for marketers. Businesses (and nonprofit institutions) need new ways to provide value to customers, particularly as competition intensifies and the need to create satisfactory, long-term relationships among manufacturers, suppliers, retailers, and customers accelerates. Today's marketing student needs to understand the producer/consumer relationship and how information technology can contribute to its changes. Today's marketing student must be a global citizen, able to transcend national boundaries—globalization means that we no longer think in terms of domestic versus foreign competition. Marketers of the future need to focus on long-term thinking as they try to anticipate and stay on top of these developments.

What makes this field exciting to you, personally, and why do you love what you do? I chose the field of marketing/consumer behavior because I am fascinated by the everyday activities of people. It is the study of how our world is influenced by the action of marketers. Since I am a consumer as well, I have a selfish interest in learning more about how this process works. In many fields, students are passive observers, learning about topics that affect them only indirectly. However, we are all consumers—everyone can relate to the trials and tribulations that consumers face—how having and not having things affects our lives and influences the way we feel about ourselves and about each other.

BEFORE YOU DECIDE . . .

Before you invest the next four years pursuing this field of study, invest a few hours in a thorough investigation of what a degree in marketing can do for you. Use the following suggestions and the worksheet at the end of this chapter to make a plan for conducting some field research. Once your plan is complete and approved by your instructor, proceed to Part 5, Field Research, where you'll find further instructions for making the most of these activities.

TALK ABOUT IT

Conduct interviews with the following three people (using the information included in the Field Research section in Part 5 of this book to guide your discussions):

- A senior completing a degree in marketing
- A marketing professor at your school
- A professional working in a marketing-related career

READ ABOUT IT

Following is a book listing that provides an overview of possible career options for someone with a degree in marketing.

- Basye, Anne and Jim Kobs. *Opportunities in Direct Marketing Careers.* Lincolnwood, IL: VGM Career Horizons, 1992.
- Camenson, Blythe. *Real People Working in Sales and Marketing.* Lincolnwood, IL: VGM Career Horizons, 1996.
- Evans, Joel R. *Careers in Marketing: Interactive Student Study Software.* New York: Macmillan College Division, 1996.
- Field, Shelly. *Career Opportunities in Advertising and Public Relations.* New York: Facts on File, 1996.
- Hird, Caroline. *Careers in Marketing, Advertising, and Public Relations.* New York: Kogan Page Ltd., 1996.
- Mogel, Leonard. *Making It in Pubic Relations.* New York: Macmillan, 1993.
- Paetro, Maxine. *How to Put Your Book Together and Get a Job in Advertising.* Chicago: The Copy Workshop, 1998.
- Pattis, William S. *Opportunities in Advertising.* Lincolnwood, IL: VGM Career Horizons, 1993.
- Rotman, Morris B. *Opportunities in Public Relations.* Lincolnwood, IL: VGM Career Horizons, 1995.
- Stair, Lila B. *Careers in Marketing.* Lincolnwood, IL: VGM Career Horizons, 1995.
- Steinberg, Margery. *Opportunities in Marketing Careers.* Lincolnwood, IL: VGM Career Horizons, 1994.

EXPERIENCE IT

Seek out an opportunity to see what a degree in marketing can do for you in the workplace. Arrange a tour, a job-shadowing experience, or even a full-fledged internship at a place such as:

- An advertising agency
- A market research firm

- The marketing department of a major corporation
- A public relations agency
- A nonprofit agency of any size
- The office of a self-employed marketing consultant

Once you have scheduled a first appointment, use the information included in the Field Research section of this book to make the most of this experience.

EXPLORE THE OPTIONS

Using the materials included in the Field Research section at the end of this book, conduct a thorough investigation of at least two career options for college graduates with a marketing degree. You'll need a good selection of career books and resources and access to the Internet to complete this task. Here are some ways to put a degree in marketing to work. Use this list for ideas but feel free to focus your exploration on another idea that interests you.

- Advertising Account Executive
- Brand Manager
- Copywriter
- Development Director
- Direct Sales Representative
- Graphic Designer
- Marketing Director
- Market Researcher
- Media Director
- Product Development Director
- Promotion Manager
- Public Relations Specialist
- Research Analyst
- Retail Sales Manager
- Salesperson
- Television Commercial Producer

REFERENCES

Evans, Joel and Barry Berman. *Principles of Marketing.* Upper Saddle River, NJ: Prentice Hall, 1995.

Solomon, Michael. *The Box: Marketing Real People, Real Choices.* Upper Saddle River, NJ: Prentice Hall, 1997.

Now that you've learned a little about what a major in marketing is like, think about what it means for you. Could this be a good choice? Can you say with reasonable certainty that it's not a good fit at all? Use the following planning worksheet to explain your response.

NO WAY!

Here are three reasons why I don't think this major would be a good choice for me.

_____

_____

_____

Stop! If you are sure this is not a major you want to pursue, don't waste another minute! Move on and explore another major.

A DEFINITE MAYBE

Here are three reasons why I think this major might be a good choice for me.

_____

_____

_____

Following are my plans to find out all I can about this major.

FIELD RESEARCH PROJECT 1: TALK ABOUT IT

I will use the materials included in the Field Research section of this book (Part 5) to conduct interviews with the following people:

_____ Senior completing a major in marketing

_____ Marketing professor

_____ Marketing professional

FIELD RESEARCH PROJECT 2: READ ABOUT IT

I will use the materials included in Part 5 of this book to review the following book(s) about potential career tracks:

_____

_____

FIELD RESEARCH PROJECT 3: EXPERIENCE IT

I have arranged a tour or job-shadowing experience at the following location and will use the materials included in Part 5 of this book to record my observations:

_____ Location

_____ Contact Person

_____ Date and Time of Appointment

FIELD RESEARCH PROJECT 4: EXPLORE THE OPTIONS

I want to find out all I can about the following career(s) and will use the materials included in Part 5 of this book to guide my investigation at the library and on the Internet:

_____ Career Choice #1

_____ Career Choice #2

_____

Student's Name and Date

_____ Field Research Plan Approved
_____ Field Research Plan Not Approved

Because:

_____

_____

_____

Instructor's Signature and Date

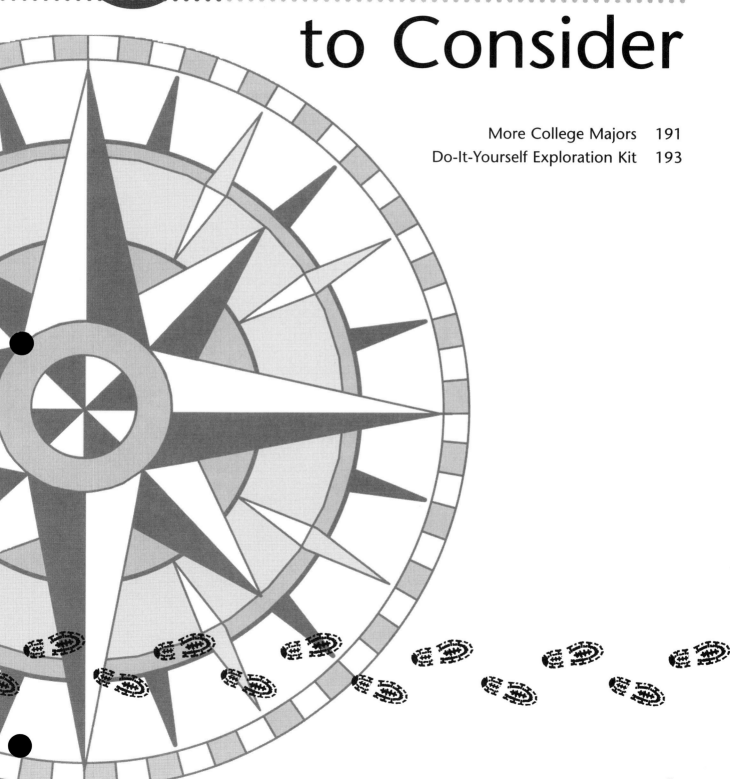

4 More Options to Consider

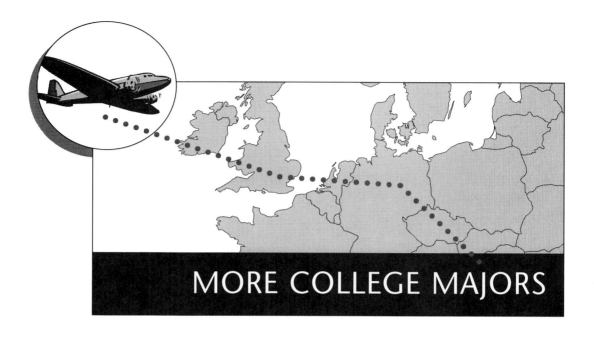

MORE COLLEGE MAJORS

What if you've looked through this entire book and still haven't found a good match for your skills, interests, values, and ambitions? Don't panic! As thorough as this resource was intended to be, there was no way to include every single possible college major—unless the publisher issued forklifts to help you carry the resulting text. Instead, the guide offers a broad overview of popular options. Just in case none of the featured majors fit the bill, you can use this Do-It-Yourself Exploration Kit to find a better match.

First, take a look at the list below and see if one of these options might fit the bill. Please note that some similar majors go by different names and that not every college will offer all of the majors listed here. Also, feel free to add your own ideas to the end of the list.

Actuarial Science	Commercial Art
Advertising and Public Relations	Communications
Agriculture	Conservation
Agronomy	Corrections
Air Traffic Control	Culinary Arts
Anatomy	Cultural Studies
Animal Science	Dairy Science
Anthropology	Dietetics
Archeology	Entrepreneurship
Architecture	Environmental Management
Astronomy	Ethics
Botany	Family and Consumer Studies
Cinematography	Farm and Ranch Management
Classics	Fashion Design
Commerce	Fashion Merchandising

Film and Media Studies
Flight Training
Folklore
Food Science
Food Service
Forensics
Forestry
Genetics
Geology
Gerontology
Government
Graphic Design
Guidance and Counseling
Health Care Management
Home Economics
Horticulture
Hospitality
Hotel and Restaurant Management
Humanities
Human Services and Resources
Industrial Arts
Interior Design
International Affairs
International Business
Journalism
Labor and Industrial Relations
Law
Legal Studies
Liberal Arts
Library Science
Linguistics
Marine Science
Mass Communication
Medical Technology
Medicine
Meteorology
Military Science
Multicultural Studies
Naval Science
Network Administration
Neuroscience

Nursing
Nutrition
Occupational Therapy
Oceanography
Optics
Paleontology
Parks and Recreation
    Management
Peace and Conflict Studies
Pharmacology
Physical Education
Physical Therapy
Planetary and Space Science
Public Management
Public Policy
Real Estate
Recreational Facilities
    Management
Rehabilitation Therapy
Religion
Robotics
Solar Technology
Special Education
Speech Pathology and Audiology
Speech Therapy
Sports Administration
Sports Management
Sports Medicine
Technical Writing
Telecommunications
Textiles
Theology
Tourism and Travel
Urban Planning
Urban Studies
Veterinary Science
Vocational Education
Wildlife Management
Women's Studies
Zoology

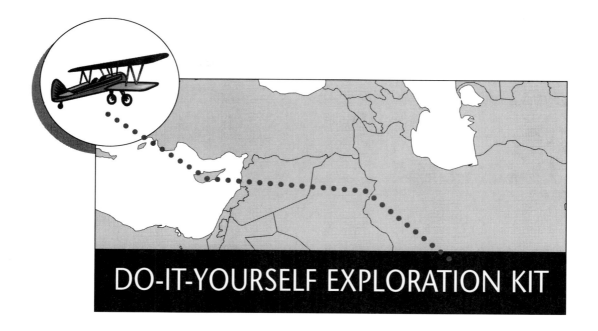

DO-IT-YOURSELF EXPLORATION KIT

Next, use the formula we've been using throughout this guide to find out all you can about the option of your choice. To do this you'll need to:

- Find a good description of the major
- Dig up some of the history and background of the major
- Find out the current status and future outlook of the major
- Take a look at the various career paths and job opportunities connected with the major
- Get some good expert advice about the major

Three resources will provide you with the information you need to make an informed decision about your college major:

THE INTERNET. Use your favorite search engine to find websites about the major in question. Use a prompt of "careers in [what the major is]" or "college degrees in [what the major is]" and you'll generally find more information than you'll be able to use. Sort through the best, follow the links provided at these sites, and you'll be well on your way to becoming an expert about these majors.

PROFESSORS AND PROFESSIONALS. If you want to know something about a particular field, the most direct route to the answer is often to ask someone who knows. In this case, talk with professors who teach courses in the major, and talk with professionals who are putting what they learned in college to work in the real world.

THE LIBRARY. Find copies of textbooks used in introductory classes, articles in professional journals, and other written resources to help fill in the blanks on any missing information.

Use the worksheets on the next pages to help you organize and record the information that you find. Make additional copies of this sheet to explore multiple majors.

WHAT IS _____?

_____

_____

_____

_____

HISTORY AND BACKGROUND

_____

_____

_____

_____

_____

_____ TODAY

_____

_____

_____

_____

_____

WHAT COURSES DO YOU NEED TO TAKE?

- _____
- _____
- _____
- _____

- _____
- _____
- _____
- _____

WHAT DO THE EXPERTS SAY ABOUT THIS MAJOR?

_____

_____

_____

_____

_____

WHAT IS _____?

_____
_____
_____
_____

HISTORY AND BACKGROUND

_____
_____
_____
_____
_____

_____ TODAY

_____
_____
_____
_____
_____

WHAT COURSES DO YOU NEED TO TAKE?

- _____   - _____
- _____   - _____
- _____   - _____
- _____   - _____

WHAT DO THE EXPERTS SAY ABOUT THIS MAJOR?

_____
_____
_____
_____

WHAT IS _____?

_____

_____

_____

_____

HISTORY AND BACKGROUND

_____

_____

_____

_____

_____

_____ TODAY

_____

_____

_____

_____

_____

WHAT COURSES DO YOU NEED TO TAKE?

- _____   - _____
- _____   - _____
- _____   - _____
- _____   - _____

WHAT DO THE EXPERTS SAY ABOUT THIS MAJOR?

_____

_____

_____

_____

5 Field Research

This is the section where you put it all together—all the facts, the "inside information," and your own perceptions about whether or not a particular major is right for you. Sure, this process may feel an awful lot like another research project. However, there's one big difference. This research project counts for more than a grade. It's your chance to sort through all the confusing choices and find direction for your future.

The Field Research Project involves completing four assignments. Here's what you'll need to do:

- **Field Research Assignment #1.**

  Talk About It consists of interviews with three people who can provide the inside scoop on what a particular major is all about—a student, a professor, and a professional.

- **Field Research Assignment #2.**

  Read About It involves reading as much as possible about the major and the opportunities for which it would prepare you. Think of it as a crash course—College Major 101—in finding out what declaring a certain major would mean in the long haul.

- **Field Research Assignment #3.**

  Experience It offers a chance to see what kinds of career paths are open to successful graduates within a particular major. It gives a picture of various careers in the real world.

- **Field Research Assignment #4.**

  Explore the Options is where you'll choose a career and find out how to make it yours.

As you work your way through this section, you'll find that there are instructions for each assignment as well as some tips for getting the most out of the process. Following the instructions are actual worksheets that you can use to complete each assignment.

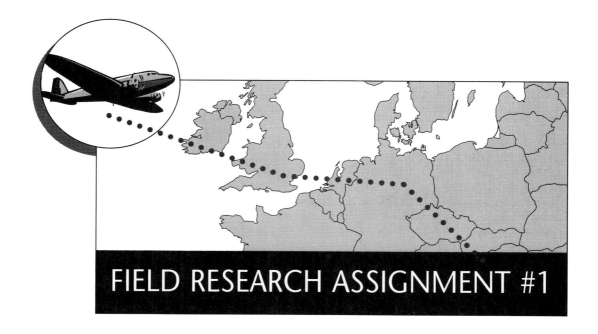

FIELD RESEARCH ASSIGNMENT #1

TALK ABOUT IT

On the next few pages you'll find worksheets to use when you conduct your interviews. Each worksheet includes a set of suggested questions. Use these and/or any others that you think of to find out all you can about the major itself and the skills you'll need to transition into a successful career.

First, take a look at these tips for conducting interviews with people who can provide the "been there, done that" type of perspective that you won't find anywhere else.

WHO are you going to interview?

Conduct interviews with the following three people:

- A senior completing a major
- A professor at your school
- A professional working in a related career

WHY are you going to interview these people?

To get an insider's perspective of what the program is like and what kinds of opportunities it provides for successful graduates.

HOW are you going to find people to interview?

Sometimes the best leads come from just asking around. You never know when "someone knows someone, who knows someone who has just the information you are looking for." If your networking efforts don't pay off, try some of these spots to find people with answers to the questions you have about your major:

- Head of the Department
- Your Student Advisor
- Student and Faculty Directories
- Alumni Directories
- Job Placement Office
- Chamber of Commerce
- Professional Associations
- Internet Connections

WHERE are you going to conduct your interviews?

Choosing where to conduct your interview obviously depends on where you are in relation to the interview subject. If you find someone engaged in interesting work in another part of the country (or world!), don't hesitate to tap into the wonders of modern technology to get in touch. Following are legitimate ways to conduct your interviews:

- On the phone
- Through the mail
- Via Internet e-mail
- In person at the interviewee's office, at a coffee shop, or other convenient location

WHEN are you going to conduct your interviews?

Agree on a time mutually convenient to you and your subject (the onus to accommodate their busy schedules is, of course, with you). Being the sensitive and considerate college student, you know to use their time with care and consideration by being on time, being prepared, and staying focused on the task at hand.

A Few Tips for a Successful Interview

- Be prepared—have pen, paper, and questions ready.
- Speak up—clearly and politely.
- Listen carefully and follow up each response with an appropriate comment or additional questions—let the conversation flow.
- Relax—most people will be flattered that you have asked them to talk about their work and will be glad to take the time to talk with you. (If you happen upon someone who isn't receptive, thank them for their time and find someone else.)
- Follow up your conversation with a thank-you note—handwritten and sincere.

If things went well, make it a point to keep in touch and let these people know how things are progressing with your program. You never know—they might become a vital link to your future success and vice versa.

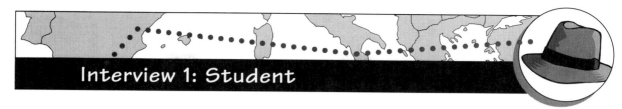

Interview 1: Student

Name _____

Address _____

Phone _____ E-mail _____

Appointment Date _____ Time _____

Place _____

SUGGESTED QUESTIONS: Be prepared! Check those that you plan to use or add your own.

- Why did you choose this major?
- When did you decide to pursue this major?
- What have you liked most about this major?
- What have you liked least about it?
- Which classes have been your favorites?
- Have you been involved in other activities that have helped?
- What do you plan to do when you graduate?
- Have you discovered any resources that helped you connect with employers in this field?
- Have any professors been especially helpful to you?
- What do I need to know to succeed in this program?

Q _____

_____

A _____

_____

_____

Q _____

_____

A _____

_____

_____

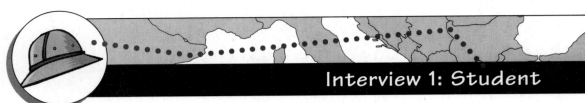

Q _____

_____

A _____

_____

_____

Q _____

_____

A _____

_____

_____

Q _____

_____

A _____

_____

_____

PERSONAL DEBRIEFING

Based on what you have learned from this person, what do you think about this college major as a possibility for you? Write your ideas in the space below.

_____

_____

_____

_____

_____

_____

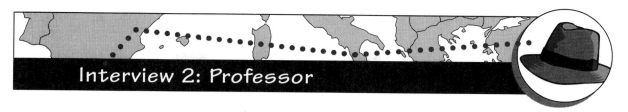

Interview 2: Professor

Name _____

Address _____

Phone _____ E-mail _____

Appointment Date _____ Time _____

Place _____

SUGGESTED QUESTIONS: Be prepared! Check those that you plan to use or add
your own.

- What classes do you teach?
- Why did you decide to teach?
- What other kinds of experience do you have in this profession?
- What kinds of things do successful students in this program have in common?
- What kind of background best prepares a student for this program?
- What kinds of opportunities are there for graduates of this program?
- What kinds of classes will I need to take?
- Are there other types of activities in which I should get involved?
- What's the best way that you can think of for someone to get firsthand experience with this major?
- How would you describe this program?

Q _____

_____

A _____

_____

_____

Q _____

_____

A _____

_____

_____

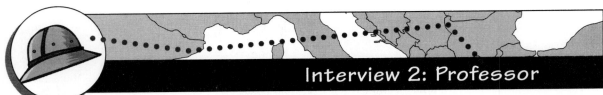
Q _____

_____

A _____

_____

_____

Q _____

_____

A _____

_____

_____

Q _____

_____

A _____

_____

_____

PERSONAL DEBRIEFING

Based on what you have learned from this person, what do you think about this college major as a possibility for you? Write your ideas in the space below.

_____

_____

_____

_____

_____

_____

Interview 3: Professional

Name _____

Address _____

Phone _____ E-mail _____

Appointment Date _____ Time _____

Place _____

SUGGESTED QUESTIONS: Be prepared! Check those that you plan to use or add your own.

- Where did you go to school and in what did you major?
- How difficult did you find the program and what kind of grades did you get?
- What is your current position and what do you do?
- How did you get this position?
- What other kinds of jobs have you had that are related to this major?
- What do you like most about your work?
- What do you like least about your work?
- What was the best preparation you received in college that has helped on the job?
- What advice do you have for someone starting out in this field?
- Have you any recommendations of organizations or activities in which I should get involved?
- If you had a chance to do it all over again, what would you do differently as a student?

Q _____

_____

A _____

_____

_____

Q _____

_____

A _____

_____

_____

Q _____

_____

A _____

_____

_____

Q _____

_____

A _____

_____

_____

Q _____

_____

A _____

_____

_____

PERSONAL DEBRIEFING

Based on what you have learned from this person, what do you think about this college major as a possibility for you? Write your ideas in the space below.

_____

_____

_____

_____

_____

_____

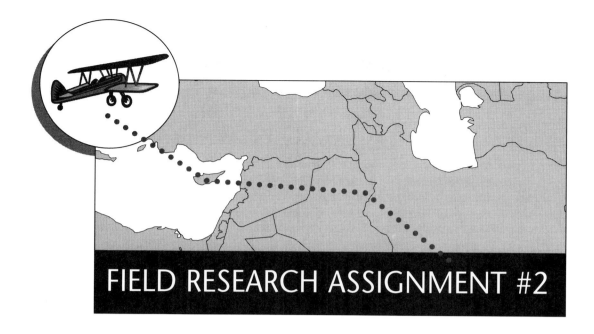

FIELD RESEARCH ASSIGNMENT #2

READ ABOUT IT

Everything you need to know about almost anything is out there—you just have to find it. Finding it and using it sums up what you'll need to do to complete this assignment. Each chapter included a list of books related to the featured major. Look for these titles and others at the library (on campus and off, if necessary) or at a bookstore (if you're interested in making a relatively small investment in your future). Your task is not necessarily to read each book from cover to cover but to scan through them and focus on information relevant to your own quest for answers.

Along with books and other more traditional resources, you may find a wealth of up-to-the-minute information on the Internet. Simply prompt a search engine to find information about "college majors" or "careers" in your area of interest.

As you go through each resource, find the following types of information in order to complete the **Read About It** book reports on the next few pages:

- Career options with a 4-year degree
- Career options with advanced degrees
- Skills needed to succeed in this field
- "Hot" areas of innovation and growth in this field
- A description of a typical workplace for someone working in this field
- Professional organizations and other resources
- Internet connections

While you are digging for all this information, stay focused on how it relates to you and your future career.

Read About It 1: Book Report

Author: _____

Title: _____

Publisher: _____ Copyright Date: _____

Number of Pages: _____ Number of Chapters: _____

- Career options with a 4-year degree _____
  _____
  _____

- Career options with advanced degrees _____
  _____
  _____

- Skills needed to succeed in this field _____
  _____
  _____

- "Hot" areas of innovation and growth in this field _____
  _____
  _____

- A description of a typical workplace for someone working in this field ___
  _____
  _____

- Professional organizations and other resources _____
  _____
  _____

- Internet connections _____
  _____

PERSONAL DEBRIEFING

Based on what you have learned from this investigation, what do you think about this college major as it relates to your career ambitions? Write your ideas in the space below.

_____

_____

_____

_____

_____

_____

_____

_____

_____

_____

_____

Read About It 2: Internet Resource (optional)

Website Name: _____

Website Adress: _____

Sponsor: _____

Webmaster: _____

- Career options with a 4-year degree _____

  _____

  _____

- Career options with advanced degrees _____

  _____

  _____

- Skills needed to succeed in this field _____

  _____

  _____

- "Hot" areas of innovation and growth in this field _____

  _____

  _____

- A description of a typical workplace for someone working in this field ___

  _____

  _____

- Professional organizations and other resources _____

  _____

  _____

- Other internet connections _____

  _____

  _____

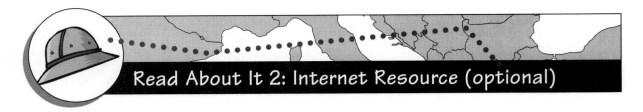

PERSONAL DEBRIEFING

Based on what you have learned from this investigation, what do you think about this college major as it relates to your career ambitions? Write your ideas in the space below.

_____

_____

_____

_____

_____

_____

_____

_____

_____

_____

_____

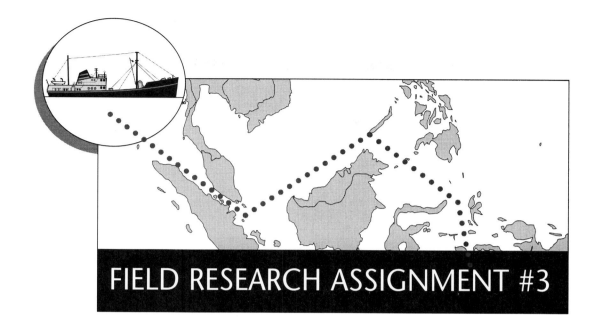

FIELD RESEARCH ASSIGNMENT #3

EXPERIENCE IT

You'll never know until you try it. Nowhere is this axiom more true than when it comes to choosing a career. Unfortunately, it's something that's all too often overlooked as people start preparing themselves for a future career. They choose a major, spend four years preparing for what sounds like an interesting career, graduate, get a job, and find out that they hate it. It's not at all what they had in mind. That's just the problem. What you "think" something is like is not necessarily what it is really like.

A workplace tour or job-shadowing experience lets you take off the blinders and see what the real world of work in a particular field is like. It's like trying on a hat to see if it fits. You get a realistic sense of whether or not you are cut out for that type of work—doing those kinds of tasks, in that kind of environment, with that type of people, etc.

All it takes to get a job-shadowing situation set up are the right connections and a phone call or two. First, ask around to see if anyone you know has the kind of job you'd like to know more about. If not, there are a few places you can look, including the:

- Yellow pages—find industries and businesses that might employ that type of professional.
- Campus job placement service—they'll know who's who among the companies that recruit students for jobs.
- Chamber of Commerce—they'll know what the resources are near your school or home.
- Professional associations—they'll be able to put you in contact with local members.

Once you've tracked down the right type of business, you'll be amazed at what a few phone calls can do, even if you don't know who to call. Just call the main number, explain to the operator what you're looking for, and take it from there.

When you've located the right person, explain what you are doing and ask if you can arrange a visit to see what their job is like. If they say yes, it's up to you to:

- Make a date and arrange the details (what time is best to visit, how long should you plan to stay, directions to the facility, etc.).
- Find out all you can about the company and the type of work the person does so you can ask intelligent questions.
- Arrive on time, dress neatly, relax, and enjoy the experience.
- Use the following pages, which include space for you to record your observations.

Experience It 1: Job-Shadowing Observations

Name _____

Title _____ Company _____

Address _____

Phone Number _____ E-mail _____

Directions to Facility _____

TAKE A PICTURE

When you arrive, take a mental picture of your surroundings. Use the space below to describe what the work environment is like, how the building and offices are organized, etc.

_____

_____

_____

_____

_____

KEEP A LOG

As best you can, keep track of everything that the person does while you are there. Make note of any phone calls, meetings, people that they interface with, tasks that they do, equipment that they use, etc.

Arrival Time: _____

- _____
- _____
- _____
- _____
- _____
- _____
- _____

Departure Time: _____

TAKE A TOUR

If you get the chance, take a tour through the facility and list all of the other kinds of jobs you see people doing. Also, record any observations of what it might be like to work for a company like this.

_____

_____

_____

_____

_____

_____

If available, pick up copies of the company's annual report and other promotional materials and attach them to this report.

PERSONAL DEBRIEFING

Can you see yourself enjoying work like this? Based on what you learned from this experience, do you think this major is a good fit for what you want to do with your life? Write your ideas in the space below.

_____

_____

_____

_____

_____

_____

_____

_____

_____

_____

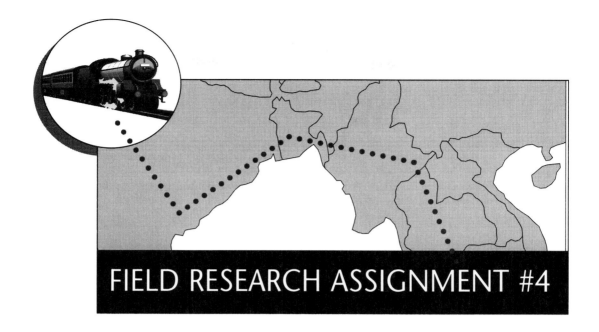

FIELD RESEARCH ASSIGNMENT #4

EXPLORE THE OPTIONS

By this time, you should be familiar with a broad array of career options related to various fields of study. Now it's time to narrow things down a bit and "get down and dirty" with the details that define a specific career track. First, pick two or three career options that appeal to you (refer to the chapter list or draw from the other research you've completed). Next, head to the library or Internet for information. You can refer to some of the resources you used for Assignment #2 or find your way to the career section of a good reference library and browse through the career "encyclopedias" and other resources for the following facts:

- Title of entry-level position
- Description of typical duties
- Potential entry-level earnings
- Job outlook
- Actual places where you might work when you graduate
- Next steps in typical career progression
- Things you can do now to boost your resume

Use the following worksheets to keep track of what you discover.

Explore the Options: Career Option 1

Title of entry-level position _____

_____

Description of typical duties _____

_____

_____

_____

_____

Potential entry-level earnings

$ _____ to $ _____ per _____

Job outlook _____

_____

_____

_____

_____

ACTUAL PLACES WHERE YOU MIGHT WORK WHEN YOU GRADUATE (INCLUDE ADDRESSES)

- _____
- _____
- _____
- _____
- _____
- _____
- _____

Explore the Options: Career Option 1

NEXT STEPS IN TYPICAL CAREER PROGRESSION

Within 3 years _____

Within 5 years _____

Within 10 years _____

THINGS YOU CAN DO NOW TO BOOST YOUR RESUME

- _____
- _____
- _____
- _____
- _____
- _____

PERSONAL DEBRIEFING

Does this sound like the kind of career you want to pursue? Based on what you have learned from this experience, what do you think about this college major as it relates to you? Write your ideas in the space below.

_____

_____

_____

_____

_____

_____

_____

_____

_____

_____

Explore the Options: Career Option 2

Title of entry-level position _____

_____

Description of typical duties _____

_____

_____

_____

_____

Potential entry-level earnings

$ _____ to $ _____ per _____

Job outlook _____

_____

_____

_____

_____

ACTUAL PLACES WHERE YOU MIGHT WORK WHEN YOU GRADUATE (INCLUDE ADDRESSES)

- _____
- _____
- _____
- _____
- _____
- _____
- _____

NEXT STEPS IN TYPICAL CAREER PROGRESSION

Within 3 years _____

Within 5 years _____

Within 10 years _____

THINGS YOU CAN DO NOW TO BOOST YOUR RESUME

- _____
- _____
- _____
- _____
- _____
- _____

PERSONAL DEBRIEFING

Does this sound like the kind of career you want to pursue? Based on what you learned from this experience, what do you think about this college major as it relates to you? Write your ideas in the space below.

_____

_____

_____

_____

_____

_____

_____

_____

_____

_____

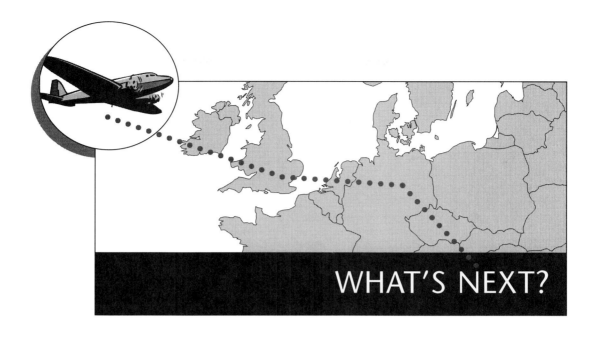

WHAT'S NEXT?

After completing this four-step process, you should have a pretty good sense of whether or not the major you investigated is a good fit with your interests, abilities, and ambitions. So, what do you think?

YES, THIS IS IT!

I plan to officially declare _____ as my major and work toward earning a degree in this area in order to pursue a career as _____.

CLOSE, BUT NOT QUITE!

I'm still really interested in the major of _____ and plan to take a few more classes and continue checking out more options before I decide for sure.

THANKS, BUT NO THANKS!

I am so glad that I went through this process because I discovered that a major in _____ is definitely not for me. I plan to use my new-found Field Research skills to start looking into other majors, such as _____.

Name _____

Date _____

INDEX